Also by the Author

Death By Chocolate

The Erin O'Reilly Mysteries
Book Seven

Steven Henry

Clickworks Press • Baltimore, MD

First publication: Clickworks Press, 2019
Release: CP-EOR7-INT-PH.IS-1.0

Sign up for updates, deals, and exclusive sneak peeks at clickworkspress.com/join.

Ebook ISBN: 978-1-943383-59-7
Paperback ISBN: 978-1-943383-60-3
Hardcover ISBN: 978-1-943383-61-0

To my father, who taught me about integrity

Death By Chocolate

Pour 1 cup crushed ice, 2 scoops chocolate ice cream, 1 ounce chocolate syrup, 1 ounce coffee liqueur, 1 ounce dark crème de cacao liqueur, and 1 ounce vodka into a blender. Blend until smooth. Pour into a stemmed glass. Garnish with whipped cream and maraschino cherry.

Chapter 1

Vic Neshenko took careful aim. Like the good rifleman he was, he knew not to rush his shot. He breathed in, held it a moment, and let the breath out slowly. Then, in that instant of perfect stillness, he took the shot.

The crumpled piece of paper ricocheted off the rim of the garbage can and bounced onto the floor of the Precinct 8 Major Crimes office.

Vic groaned and sagged in his chair.

"That's game," Erin O'Reilly said. "Five to four. Next case we close, you're buying the first round."

Erin's partner Rolf let out a long, slow sigh. He lay next to her desk on an old, folded blanket. The German Shepherd had his snout between his paws. His eyes were half-closed and unfocused. It was a slow, sleepy afternoon.

Lieutenant Webb, their commanding officer, twirled a cigarette between his fingers. They were in a city-owned facility, so smoking wasn't allowed. The cig wasn't lit. He clearly wished it was.

"Will someone, for God's sake, get murdered?" Vic asked the ceiling. "I'm bored out of my skull."

"I think New York's seen enough people murdered in the name of God," Webb said dryly. "Unless you're hoping for some more terrorists?"

"Murder's usually more personal," Erin added.

"I'd take it personal," Vic said, "if anyone murdered me."

"How're your fives coming along?" Webb asked Erin.

"Just about done."

Webb was talking about the DD-5, an infamous piece of NYPD paperwork used to add detail to a complaint report. "If it's not on a five, it didn't happen," was a common phrase in Erin's old precinct down in Queens. Filling one out wasn't her favorite use of an afternoon.

"It's okay to admit you're just looking at porn," Vic said.

"Okay, you caught me," she said, putting up her hands. "Sergeant Brown pointed me at this great website, it's got these Russian girls on it, there's one here who looks like your mom."

Vic gave her a false smile and showed her one of his fingers.

"The week after Valentine's Day," Webb said, leaning back in his chair. "And love is still in the air."

"What'd you do for the holiday?" Erin asked Vic.

"I drank. Alone."

"That reminds me," Webb said. "My alimony's coming due. I better get a check in the mail."

"How about you, Erin?" Vic asked. "You have any lights and sirens?"

"Wouldn't you love to know."

"I would," he said. "It'd give me a nice, warm image to get me through February. It's a Russian month. Dark, cold, nothing to do but drink."

"And March is like February's hangover," Webb added.

"C'mon, Erin," Vic said. "At least one of us gold shields oughta be getting some. I know I didn't get laid, and the Lieutenant, well, just look at him. So that leaves you. Did you take one for the team?"

Erin shook her head. "I'll never talk."

"I knew it!" Vic said triumphantly. "I'm thinking drunken hookup at that Irish bar she hangs out at."

"The one full of wiseguys?" Webb asked.

At that moment, Webb's phone rang. Erin felt a rush of relief as the Lieutenant took the call. Her fellow detectives had been getting a little too close to the mark. She had been with someone on Valentine's Day, and it was a man they definitely wouldn't approve of.

"Your prayers are answered," Webb announced, standing up. "We got a body."

Vic jumped to his feet. "Now that's what I'm talking about."

Rolf, catching the sudden energy in the room, scrambled to his feet and looked expectantly at Erin. She grabbed his leash and clipped it to his collar.

"Where we going, sir?" she asked Webb.

"Dentist's office," he said, deadpan.

Vic's shoulders slumped. "I knew it was too good to be true. I hate going to the dentist."

* * *

The crime scene was in Greenwich Village, in a building overlooking Washington Square Park. Erin parked her Dodge Charger next to a pair of squad cars and the coroner's van. Vic and Webb were close behind in their Taurus.

"Looks like we're late," Vic muttered. "Maybe they'll at least have some good magazines in the waiting room."

"I doubt it," Erin said. "I mean, it's usually Good Housekeeping, Better Homes and Gardens, maybe Seventeen or Cosmo. What sort of thing do you read?"

Vic shrugged. "Guns and Ammo. Soldier of Fortune."

"Surprised?" Webb asked Erin.

It was her turn to shrug. "I'm just surprised he knows how to read."

They showed their shields to a uniformed officer in the lobby and took the elevator to the sixth floor. Another uniform was guarding a door labeled "Norman Ridgeway, DDS."

"That's our victim?" Erin asked.

"We'll see in a minute," Webb said. "Dispatch just told me we had a sudden death."

"Must've been suspicious for them to call in Major Crimes right away," Vic said.

"Either that, or they heard you were bored," Webb said.

The waiting room was populated by two patients, an oral hygienist, and a secretary. The hygienist was sniffling into a tissue. One patient was a young man, college age, who was leafing through a back issue of People Magazine. The other was a thirtysomething businesswoman who looked pissed off.

"Excuse me," the businesswoman said, standing up. "I don't know who you think you are, but I've been waiting here almost forty-five minutes. This is totally unacceptable."

"I'm Lieutenant Webb," Webb said. "Major Crimes. We'll need a statement from you, but I hope you won't be inconvenienced much longer."

The woman made an exasperated sound in her nose. "I don't see how this day could possibly get any worse."

"You could've been the victim instead of a witness," Vic offered. "That'd probably be worse."

She glared at him. He gave her his best meeting-the-public smile.

"The victim's in his office," the cop at the door offered, pointing past the front desk.

Erin steered Rolf past the bystanders to the office. She'd been a cop almost twelve years. She'd responded to calls for gruesome traffic accidents, homicides, suicides, and bodies that had been dead for days by the time they were reported. Her last big, dramatic case had featured a victim literally sawed in half. She was ready for anything.

It was an anticlimax. The victim was sprawled on a leather couch against his office wall. He didn't have a mark on him. His lips were tinged blue, and there were flecks of foam at the corners of his mouth, but otherwise, he didn't look half bad. There was one odd thing about the body, however.

"Where's his clothes?" she asked aloud.

"The paramedics reported the body was this way when they arrived," a woman said. She was kneeling beside the naked corpse, dressed in a white lab coat and disposable gloves.

"Hi, Levine," Erin said, recognizing the medical examiner for their precinct. "You got here fast."

"Not particularly," Sarah Levine said. "I considered the cause of death potentially suspicious."

"That's why they called us," Vic said, coming up behind Erin. "Hey, doc. He's dead, but I bet his teeth are in fantastic condition."

Levine blinked. "I haven't examined his dentition," she said. "When there's no question of positive identification of the victim, it's not a priority."

"You have a preliminary COD?" Webb asked, moving past his detectives into the room.

"Discoloration of the lips and fingernails," Levine said. "Cyanosis, typical of asphyxia. I don't see evidence of an independent cardiac event. The lack of ligature marks on the throat indicates a probable chemical cause. The most likely agent is cyanide."

Erin glanced around the room. She saw a desk with a computer on it, an office chair behind the desk, and a coffee table. On the table was an open candy box.

"Happy Valentine's Day," she murmured.

Webb and Vic followed her look. "I wouldn't eat those," Webb said. "I'm guessing they might kill you."

"And give you cavities," Vic added.

Levine leaned forward and carefully parted the corpse's lips with a pair of gloved fingers. "Trace amounts of a brown substance between the canines and lodged in the molars," she announced. "This supports the hypothesis of toxic candy."

"I told you to check the teeth," Vic said triumphantly.

"So," Erin said. "Who was in here with him?"

"Maybe he liked eating chocolate alone," Vic said.

"Naked?" Webb asked, raising an eyebrow.

"Hey, this is New York City," Vic said. "We got all types here."

"Given the options in the waiting room," Erin said, "I'm guessing the oral hygienist."

"Not the skirt with the bad attitude?" Webb asked.

"I'm thinking the one who's crying is more likely," she replied.

He sighed. "Okay, we better talk to her." Talking to family and friends of victims was part of the Job, but no cop liked doing it.

*   *   *

They didn't want to take statements in the dental office with the dead guy, or in front of the other witnesses, so they ended up using one of the examining rooms. Erin thought it was a little weird to be interviewing a person of interest who was sitting in a dental chair, but it was hardly the strangest thing she'd done in her time with the NYPD.

The hygienist, a pretty blonde named Amber Hayward, carried a crumpled tissue in one hand. She kept dabbing at her eyes with it. Her mascara was running.

"Miss Hayward," Webb said, "can you tell us what happened?"

"I came in to work," Amber said. "Well, I had breakfast before that. And before that, I put on my makeup. And my clothes. And got out of bed. I guess I woke up first."

"Take your time," Webb said.

"The first appointment was at nine," she went on. "That was Mr. Pavlicek, with his root canal. It was the number nineteen molar. Doctor Ridgeway decided to do a standard procedure, with..."

Webb held up a hand. "I don't think we need the details of the procedure," he said. "Maybe you could skip ahead a little."

Amber nodded. "After Mr. Pavlicek, we had three more appointments. Teddy Coogan, extraction of a dead baby tooth, that was tooth 5D. Then Paul Dexter, impacted wisdom tooth, number sixteen. And Lori Smithers, routine exam and cleaning, just before lunch."

"Does anyone else work in the office?" Webb asked.

"Nelda Booker, our other hygienist," Amber said. "And Della Ackerman, our secretary."

"Where's Nelda?" Vic asked.

"Out to lunch," Amber said. "She'll be back any minute. Oh God, what am I going to tell her?" She blew her nose loudly.

"What happened at lunchtime?" Webb asked.

"We had an hour and a half blocked out on the schedule," she said. "Nelda went to meet her mom. Mrs. Booker works for a Wall Street firm. They have lunch together once a week. Norm... Doctor Ridgeway, I mean... he said we'd have time to eat... later."

"Miss Hayward," Webb said quietly, "were you and Doctor Ridgeway physically intimate?"

Amber nodded and whimpered.

"Amber," Erin said. "Where did the chocolates come from?"

The hygienist's eyes filled with new tears. "I gave them to him!" she wailed. "I put... I put one... right in his mouth! And then he started gasping, and his face went blue! I killed him! Oh God, I killed him!"

"Well, this'll be a short case," Vic whispered in Erin's ear.

She ignored him. "Amber," she asked the young woman, "was the box opened?"

"What?" Amber sniffled.

"When you went to give Doctor Ridgeway the chocolates, had the box been opened previously?"

"I... I don't understand."

Erin knew it was important to be patient during witness interviews. "Was the box wrapped? With plastic?"

"Oh. No."

"Were any chocolates missing, or disturbed?"

"Yes," Amber said. "It wasn't a full box. Maybe four or five were missing. Rocky said he ate a few. It's so typical of him. Even a gift, he just can't help himself."

"Who's Rocky?" Webb asked sharply.

"Rocky Nicoletti," she said. "My... my boyfriend."

Webb's eyebrows went up. "Your boyfriend," he echoed in a flat voice.

She nodded. Then a thought hit her. "Oh my God. He might have eaten... he might be... oh God. Rocky!" Then she started crying again.

Erin exchanged glances with Vic. He shrugged. Rolf, at Erin's side, was the only one who wasn't surprised. To him, most human interactions were nonsensical. He kept watching his partner, in case she decided to do something more up his alley.

"Miss Hayward," Webb said. "Were you and Doctor Ridgeway getting along?"

"Wha... what?" she snuffled.

"Had you been fighting?" he asked gently. "Was he putting pressure on you to do something you didn't want to?"

Amber shook her head. "No! Norm... Norm's a sweetheart. He's kind and... and good with kids. He talked about dinosaurs with Teddy Coogan!"

"So you weren't angry at him?" Webb pressed.

Erin saw recognition hit Amber. "You think *I* wanted to hurt him?" Amber exclaimed. "You think I took a box of chocolates, and... and poisoned them... and gave one... to my Normie?"

"Normie?" Vic said, but he said it quietly and no one took any notice of him.

"You..." Amber advanced on Webb, waving her used tissue in his face. "You... you big jerk!" She threw the soggy scrap of paper at him. It bounced off his trench coat and landed on the carpet. Then Amber buried her face in her hands and sobbed.

Webb didn't react. If a cop didn't get called something worse than "jerk," it was a good day on the Job.

"Amber," Erin said gently. "Rocky gave you the chocolates?"

It took a moment to get through to her, and she had to repeat the question, but the other woman finally nodded.

"Were they a Valentine's Day gift?" Erin asked.

Amber nodded again.

"Amber," she said. "Please listen. This is important. Did Rocky know about Norm?"

"I... I don't... I don't know," Amber managed to say between hiccupping sobs. Then she lost whatever was left of her self-control and became useless from a police perspective.

Erin cocked her head to Webb and Vic. They stepped into the hallway just outside the examining room.

"What do you think?" Webb asked his two detectives.

"If she's a murderer," Vic said, "I'll field-strip my gun and eat it, one piece at a time."

"I'm with Vic," Erin said. "I don't even think Ridgeway was the intended target."

"It does seem like a pretty iffy way to kill someone," Webb said. "You think it was meant for Miss Hayward?"

Erin nodded. "If she's telling the truth, and Rocky gave them to her..."

"Then Rocky's got some explaining to do," Vic finished for her.

Chapter 2

Rocky Nicoletti's address was in Little Italy, in one of the nicer apartments in the area. Webb had looked him up on the way over. What he'd found was a little surprising.

"He's connected," Webb said.

"To whom?" Erin asked.

"The Lucarellis."

Vic whistled. "I didn't know we'd be tangling with the Mafia when I got out of bed this morning. I'd have worn my good suit."

"The Mafia?" Erin repeated. "Seriously?"

Webb didn't look like he was joking. "This kid's got a jacket," he said. "Mostly small-time, but he's a known associate of some heavy hitters. His uncle is Marco Nicoletti, alias Broken Nose Nicky, otherwise known as Nicky the Nose."

"I don't know him," Erin said.

"Neither do I," Vic said. "But I bet I could pick him out of a lineup."

"Your nose is broken, too," she reminded him.

He put a hand to his face. "Yeah, but if I had a Mafia nickname, I'd be 'Vic the Russky,' or some shit like that."

"Nicky the Nose is a leg-breaker for the Lucarelli Family," Webb explained, trying to pull them back on task. "He's currently doing a dime upstate, attempted murder."

"What about the kid?" Erin asked.

"Rocky Nicoletti," Webb recited. "Birth name Rocco, age twenty. Did a stint in Juvie, arson. Set fire to his junior high school bathroom, nearly burned down the school. Got expelled, as you might expect. He's been in and out of trouble since. Lots of petty theft, harassment, that sort of thing."

"Sounds like a real solid citizen," Vic said. "What're we waiting for? Let's haul his ass downtown."

"He may not even be home," Erin said.

"Won't know until we try," Webb said.

*   *   *

The detectives lined up at Rocky's eighth-floor apartment. They weren't serving a warrant, and there was no reason to expect trouble, but Erin and Vic both had their hands on their sidearms when Webb knocked on the door. If Nicoletti was a mobster, there was no telling who might be inside, or what he might do when the cops came calling.

"Hey, Rocky Nicoletti!" Webb shouted. "This is the NYPD! Come on out. We want to talk to you."

There was no answer.

Webb gave it a few seconds and tried again. "Nicoletti!" he called, a little louder than before.

"The hell do you want?" a groggy voice mumbled from the other side of the door.

"Open up. It's the NYPD."

The voice suggested something Webb could do with his mother.

"You coming out, or are we coming in?" Webb retorted. It

was a bluff. They didn't have a warrant or probable cause. If the Lieutenant broke the door down, he'd also be breaking the law.

Erin suspected Rocky knew that perfectly well. But either he was too sleepy to think straight, or he didn't think he had anything to fear, because the door opened a few inches. An unshaven face peered out at them with bloodshot eyes.

"Who the hell are you?" the guy demanded.

Webb held up his shield. "Lieutenant Webb, NYPD. You Rocky?"

"Goddamn cops," Rocky muttered. "I didn't do nothin.""

"We just need to ask you a few questions," Webb said. "It's about your girlfriend, Amber Hayward."

"I told you, I didn't—" he began, then stopped. "What about her?"

"When's the last time you saw her?" Webb asked.

Rocky's eyes cleared a little. Erin could see him waking up, becoming wary. "Why you wanna know?"

"She's a person of interest in a serious situation," Webb said. "I'm hoping you can help us clear things up. Can we come in?"

Rocky thought it over for a second. Erin could practically read his thoughts. He was going through a checklist of what they'd see in his apartment, debating with himself whether he'd get in trouble for any of it. Then he shrugged.

"Sure." He caught sight of Rolf. "But not the dog."

"Why not?" Erin challenged.

"I got allergies." He sniffled loudly and rubbed his nose.

"He stays with me," she said.

"Then you stay in the hallway."

Erin sighed. "Kiddo, he's trained in bomb detection and suspect apprehension. As long as you're not building pipe bombs or kidnapping people, we've got no problem."

"Okay, whatever," Rocky said, rubbing his nose again. Erin

was pretty sure she saw white, powdery residue on his nostrils.

Rocky was half-dressed, in boxer shorts and a wife-beater. His hair was uncombed and he could definitely use a shower. His apartment was a bachelor pad. The most expensive things in it were the gaming console and TV in the living room. Erin scanned the place with an experienced policewoman's eye. She didn't see any weapons or obvious stashes of drugs, but she did see the mirror on the coffee table, and she'd bet the residue on it wasn't powdered sugar. Rocky was definitely a drug user.

If Webb saw it, he didn't give any sign. "Tell us about Amber," he said.

"What about her?" Rocky asked. "We hang out sometimes. Sure, she was over here. It was Valentine's Day, you know how it is, man."

"I know how it is," Vic said. "You spend the day with the people you love, holding hands, getting high, eating chocolates."

"Hey, I don't know what you're talkin' about," Rocky said.

"Did you give her anything?" Webb asked.

Rocky grinned, his eyes going to Erin. "Oh yeah, I gave her plenty."

She resisted the urge to roll her eyes. For some reason, a female cop made guys like him want to brag about their conquests. But she'd heard it all before.

"We're talking about gifts," she said, ignoring his tone.

"Oh, yeah," he said. "I gave her a box of chocolate."

Webb showed a hint of surprise. Erin felt the same way. They hadn't expected him to admit it so easily.

"I'm going to have to ask you to come down to the station with us," the Lieutenant said.

It was Rocky's turn to look surprised. "What for? Chocolate's not against the law!"

"No," Webb agreed. "But murder is."

"Murder?" Rocky repeated, eyes going wide. "You're batshit!

I didn't kill nobody!"

"I've got a dead body in a dentist's office that says otherwise," Webb said. He pulled out his handcuffs. "I think you know them already, you've sure heard them enough times, but I'm going to advise you of your rights."

Erin and Vic tensed, just in case Rocky tried to run or fight. But he'd been through the system enough times to know better.

"Can I put on some clothes?" he asked. "And shoes?"

Webb nodded. "Neshenko, keep an eye on him."

"You might want to pack a toothbrush, while you're at it," Vic suggested. "You might be staying overnight."

* * *

By the time they got Rocky into the interrogation room, he'd had a chance to recover a little of his composure. He was smiling in a cocky way, even swaggering a little. He'd been in plenty of police stations before, and he'd usually walked out of them again. He wasn't scared, and he wanted them to know it.

Erin and Webb went into the room with him, while Vic waited outside. Erin had learned that young punks tended to be more talkative in the presence of an attractive woman, and Webb, always pragmatic, was willing to use that for all it was worth.

"So, Rocky," Erin said. "You know how to treat a girl. I can tell."

He smirked. "You know it, lady."

"The chocolates weren't the first thing you gave Amber," Erin went on. "What does she like? Is she a jewelry girl? Flowers?"

"Hey, you know, it's all sorts of shit," Rocky said. "The main thing is, you gotta show you're thinking about 'em, and you gotta spend money on 'em. See, the more you spend, the more you care, right? It's, like, mathematical."

Erin nodded, keeping a straight face. "You spend a lot on Amber, don't you?"

"Oh yeah. Hey, I take her out to a restaurant, it's not McDonald's, right? No, we're talking Angelo's on Mulberry, shrimp cocktails, salad, main course, hundred-dollar champagne. The good stuff, y'know? I'm spending, like, three hundred there. Cash!"

Webb gave Erin a slight nod to keep going. As long as Rocky was talking, the interrogation was a success. Erin's dad had given her some advice about interrogating suspects back when she'd first started on the Job.

"Everybody's got a story they tell themselves. Sure, it's a bunch of lies, but it's what they say in their own heads. Even the lies tell you things. What you gotta do is, you gotta get them to tell you their story."

"She's a lucky girl," Erin said, smiling at Rocky. "You give her any special treats like you have at your apartment?"

A crafty look came into Rocky's eyes. "Hey, I don't know nothin' about that," he said. "I'm no dealer."

"You seeing anybody besides her?" she asked.

The smirk came back to his face. "Hey, she's my special girl, but what am I supposed to do? Some hot chick throws herself at me, you know how it is. I got needs, right?"

"She seeing anybody else?" Erin asked.

"No!"

Erin saw the flash of anger, the sudden defensiveness. Webb saw it, too. He sat forward slightly, watching Rocky more closely.

"You sure about that?" Webb challenged him.

"Why would she?" he shot back. "Hey, I was giving her everything a girl needs. And I mean, everything. I know how to keep a girl satisfied!"

"Yeah," Erin agreed. "All that money, those nice dinners,

presents, maybe even a little nose candy. Plus, having a hot guy like you? I don't know why she'd hook up with her boss. Ridgeway's not even that good-looking."

"No shit," Rocky snorted. "I dunno what she sees in that asshole. I gave her everything. Everything! And what's she do? And then, when I found out about it, you know what she told me?"

"What?" Erin made her face into a mask of concerned curiosity.

"She said, 'He knows how to treat a girl!'" Rocky said in disbelief. "Like what I was doing didn't mean shit to her! That bitch!"

"So you gave her the chocolates," Erin said quietly.

"Yeah!"

"To teach her a lesson."

"Yeah!"

"Where'd you get the poison?"

Rocky's eyes opened suddenly wider. "Poison? What the hell do you mean, poison?"

"In the chocolates," Webb said, entering the conversation. "You wanted to kill Amber."

"What? No!" Rocky shook his head violently. "No, man! It's not like that!"

"What is it, then?" Erin asked, keeping her voice soft and reassuring. Webb was playing bad cop, so she'd play good cop. They'd done it enough times that they didn't need to discuss it.

"I saw something online, about how chicks dig the little gestures, right? And I had this box of chocolates, almost full, I thought maybe she'd like them. Maybe she'd see I really like her, y'know? And then she'd ditch that asshat Ridgeway, him and his phony white teeth. You know, I bet he uses whitening strips."

Rocky paused for breath, and Erin could see the wheels turning in his brain. He wasn't the brightest bulb in New York, but he'd finally put two and two together.

"Oh, shit. Poison? *Poison?* For real?"

"Oh, yeah," Webb said. "As real as it gets. You're looking at twenty to life, buddy. If you're lucky."

"Oh shit, man," Rocky said, and all the swagger and smirk slipped away. Erin almost felt sorry for him when she saw the naked pain in his eyes. "You mean she's dead? Amber's dead? And I killed her? The candy was... oh, man. Oh, God. And I gave it to her?"

"It's a little late to feel sorry," Webb said remorselessly. "Where'd you get the poison?"

"I didn't know!" Rocky said. "Jesus, I *ate* some of those! It might've been me! I loved Amber! I'd never... oh God..." His face twisted and big tears started rolling down his cheeks. He snuffled and wiped at his nose, burying his face in his hands.

"Amber's not dead," Erin said. He didn't seem to hear her, so she said it again, louder. "She's not dead, Rocky. She's fine."

Rocky raised his head and looked blearily at her. "You're not screwing with me, are you?"

"No, she's not," Webb said. "But Ridgeway's still dead, and you're still in a lot of trouble."

"Hey, man, I didn't know!" Rocky said. "Hell, the candy wasn't even mine!"

"Where'd you get it?" Webb demanded.

"Paulie Bianchi! He gave it to me!" Rocky froze. "I mean, it was just, like, a spur of the moment thing. Like, he just had them lying around."

"Who's Paulie Bianchi?"

"Nobody! A friend!"

Webb smiled grimly. "You sure he's your friend, Rocky? Because from where I'm sitting, it looks a whole lot like he screwed you."

"No way," Rocky said. "Paulie and me, we're tight. He's

stand-up."

"Yeah, we'll see about that," Webb said. He got out of his chair. "We're going to take a break. Take it easy, kid."

"So, can I go now?"

The Lieutenant shook his head. "You're not going anywhere."

Chapter 3

"Paulie Bianchi," Vic read off his computer screen. "The Narcs love this guy. He's been busted four times for possession, twice more for intent to distribute. Felony volume."

"What's the substance?" Webb asked.

"Cocaine the first two," Vic replied. "The others were for heroin."

"How much time did he get?" Erin asked.

"Probation," Vic said.

"The hell," she said. "We nail this guy as a drug dealer, *twice*, and he doesn't get jail time? For heroin and coke?"

Vic shrugged. "Guess he had a good lawyer."

"Or good connections," Webb said. "Do you have any known associates?"

Vic checked the database. "Rocky Nicoletti," he deadpanned.

"Besides him." Webb matched the dry tone.

"Well, his dad's old-school Mafia," Vic said.

Webb blinked. "You serious, Neshenko?"

"No joke, sir. Paulie's old man is Lorenzo Bianchi, AKA Sewer Pipe."

"It really say that?" Erin asked, walking to peer over Vic's shoulder.

"Yeah," he said. "Guess he was on a bathroom break when they were handing out nicknames."

"What've we got on Sewer Pipe?" Webb asked.

Vic was already looking. "He went upstate for a nickel on some sort of sanitation scam back in the '90s. There's a couple assault charges, weapons possession. Bianchi's been in and out of prison half his life. He's a bad guy."

"So is his son, from the sound of it," Erin said. "Let's go bring the kid in."

"Hold on," Webb said. "If this boy's connected, we need to take our time a little. This could get political."

"Great," Vic muttered.

"Neshenko, I want you to get on the phone with our friends at the FBI."

"I don't have any friends at the FBI."

"You know what I mean," Webb said. "Find out if the Feebies have anything going on with Bianchi. We don't want to step on any toes. Suppose we haul this loser's ass downtown and it spoils some big RICO sting. Then the PC calls up Captain Holliday and reams him out, the Captain tears me a new one, and I have to chew you out, and so on down the line. I don't need the heartburn. Let's take our time on this, feel things out."

"Sir," Erin said, "this doesn't feel like a mob hit."

"Of course not," Webb agreed. "The Mafia doesn't whack people with poisoned candy. They shoot you in the head. But they're involved, and I don't like it. Bianchi's been in the system longer than I've been wearing a shield. If we go in unprepared, he and his boy will lawyer up so fast your head will spin. And we don't have anything on them, yet. Just the word of a junkie whose girlfriend was screwing the victim. You think that'll hold up in court? We won't even get an indictment. So we take our time. It's just about quitting time in the private sector. Go home, see your families, get a good night's sleep for once."

"My family doesn't recognize me anymore," Vic said.

"That's just since the last time you got your nose broken," Erin said.

He grinned. "You should see the other guy."

*   *   *

That was how Erin found herself leaving the precinct at a civilized hour for the first time in a long while. In the parking garage, she loaded Rolf into her Charger, then took out her phone and dialed an unlabeled contact. It was a call to a burner cell, the sort of disposable phone favored by criminals.

"Evening, darling," the man on the other end of the line said in a distinct Northern Irish accent.

"Evening," she said. "Guess what? I'm off work early."

"That's grand," he said. "And what exactly were you planning on doing with your unexpected free time?"

"I was thinking of going home, having a nice, relaxing shower, taking it easy, maybe getting some takeout for dinner."

"And would these plans be solitary, or would you be wanting company?"

She smiled to herself. "I'll be home in half an hour," she said. "You want to come looking, you know where to find me."

Exactly thirty minutes later, there was a knock at Erin's apartment door. She'd just finished walking Rolf and was giving him his supper. The apartment had a lock on the outer door, but Morton Carlyle wasn't the sort of man to let something like that stand in his way. There he was in the hallway, a slender, handsome man, impeccably dressed, with silver hair and intensely blue eyes. He had a bottle of wine in one hand and a paper bag in the other.

"I hope you've no objection to Italian," he said with a smile.

"C'mon in," she said, stepping back from the door and holstering her Glock.

"Still answering the door with your revolver, I see."

"A serial killer tried to take me out last year," she reminded him. "I can't believe you don't carry, after all the shit that's happened to you."

"I'm not licensed. One of New York's finest, encouraging me to break the law? I believe that's called entrapment." He set the bag and bottle on the kitchen counter. "As I recall, you've a fondness for spaghetti, with meatballs."

"Everyone likes spaghetti," she said, but she was secretly pleased. They'd gone out for Italian only once, almost a month ago, and he'd remembered her order. That was Carlyle. He didn't miss much, and never forgot anything.

"If you're ready, we can set the table," he said.

"I actually still need to shower," she said. "I just got home."

"Not to worry," he said. "I'll get things ready, pour the wine."

"You could do that," she said, giving him a smile. "Or you could join me."

He returned the smile. "I suppose the food can keep a few minutes."

*　　*　　*

"I don't suppose you've heard of Lorenzo Bianchi?" Erin asked, later.

They were sitting at her small dining table, spaghetti in front of her, Carlyle with a plate of gnocchi. Rolf lay at Erin's feet, keeping an eye on Carlyle. She'd accepted him, so the K-9 did too, but the dog wanted the Irishman to know he'd better keep in line.

Carlyle raised an eyebrow. "Old Sewer Pipe? I know him, aye. That is to say, I know of him. We've not met face to face, and I doubt he'd think of me as a friend."

"Some bad blood?"

"Something of the sort."

"What can you tell me about him?"

Carlyle took a sip of his Chianti. "The lad came up through his family in Brooklyn, in the sanitation business. He handled a few dustmen's lorries."

It took her a second to translate. "Garbage trucks?"

"Aye."

"Bianchi was part of the Garbage War, back in the '90s," Erin said, remembering something her father had told her about Carlyle. "That was when you were getting started with the O'Malleys. Did you blow up Bianchi's trucks?"

"There's no statute of limitations on arson, darling," he said gently. "Are you certain you're wanting to ask me that?"

Erin shook her head. "No one got hurt in any of those bombings." She knew, because she'd checked. It was the one series of crimes she was sure Carlyle had been involved in, and when they'd started seeing each other, she'd had to know. He'd been a suspect in half a dozen truck bombings, but all of them had happened at night, in deserted parking lots. The O'Malleys had been trying to put their competitors out of business, but as Carlyle had explained to Erin once before, blood was an expense best avoided. He'd taken pains not to hurt anyone. At least, that was what she told herself.

"Right now, I just want to know about Bianchi," she said, steering clear of the subject of Carlyle's past activities. "His name got brought up in a case."

"My understanding is that he's not particularly active on the street," Carlyle said. "If you're investigating a murder, I'd be astonished to find him involved. He's somewhat older than I am, darling. Street crime is a young hoodlum's game."

Erin nodded. "Can you find out if he knows anything about poisons?"

His eyebrows went up again. "I'll see what I can discover. While we're on the subject of hobnobbing with my associates, there's a small matter I'd like to discuss."

"What's that?"

"Evan phoned me just after you called this evening. He's suggested a sit-down at the Corner. He'd like to invite you to attend."

Erin's stomach tightened. Evan O'Malley was Carlyle's boss, the head of the family. She'd never met him in person.

"Was that an order he gave you?" she asked.

"He phrased it as a request," Carlyle said.

"When?"

"Tomorrow night. Eight o'clock."

"That soon?"

"He doesn't like his movements known terribly far in advance," Carlyle said. "It'll be an informal gathering. We'll use the back room. It'll be a social gathering, an evening of cards."

"What kind of cards?"

"Evan's quite fond of poker. Texas hold 'em, specifically. You needn't be concerned about the wagering. I'll be happy to stake you."

She stared at him. "Let me get this straight," she said. "You want me to play poker with a mob boss?"

"And his lieutenants," he said. "And myself, of course. I imagine most of the others will attend, too. You'll know Corky, naturally. Then there'll be Mickey, Liam, and maybe Veronica. And Finnegan."

"Why are we doing this?" she asked.

"You know perfectly well," he replied. "As long as we're peddling the fiction that you're my source within the department, Evan wants to get a look at you. Cards are his way of taking the measure of a lad, or a lass."

"And you think this is a good idea?"

"I think it's necessary. I've managed to postpone this meeting as long as I can, getting him used to the idea of you. I've prepared the way as much as I can. Now it's time to see the thing through."

Erin shook her head. "You remember I'm not actually working for the O'Malleys, right?"

"Oh aye," he said. He paused to take a bite of gnocchi and another sip of wine. "You do know the best way to lie, don't you?"

"What's that?"

He looked her straight in the eye. "Don't. Tell the truth. Tell all the truth you can."

"And let the other guy fill in the blanks with what he wants to believe," she agreed. "But you're better at it than I am. You make it look easy."

"There's nothing easy about it, darling," he said. "I'd be lying myself if I told you there was no chance of trouble. Some of the most dangerous folk I know will be in that room. But you'll have allies, too. Corky's in my corner, and I'll watch your back. We'll manage it, no fear."

She smiled a little shakily. "This is making me wonder if this whole thing is worth it."

"Meaning me? Us?" He reached across the table and caressed her cheek. Her skin tingled at his touch. "Surely you don't mean that."

"No," she said, but a little part of her still wondered.

*　　*　　*

That night, after Carlyle had gone home, Erin lay in bed and tried to think. Rolf was curled up at her feet, but the bed felt empty. Six weeks, and she still wasn't even sure what to call the thing she had with Carlyle. An affair? A fling? He said he loved her, and to Erin's knowledge, he'd never told her an outright lie, but even if that was true, was it enough?

They were playing an extremely dangerous game. They'd agreed there were two ways to satisfy his colleagues. The first was to pretend he'd turned her, made her into a dirty cop on the O'Malley payroll. She'd never taken money from Carlyle, but money laundering was one of his jobs in the O'Malleys, and she knew he could cook the books a little further so it looked like she was getting payoffs. To keep up the fiction, she could feed the Irish Mob little tidbits of information, and make sure their rivals went down. The other option was to play the part of a lovesick woman whose head had been turned by a handsome Irishman.

They'd decided to focus on that angle. It had the advantage of being mostly true. However, it was also riskier, in that the other O'Malleys might not buy it. No wonder they wanted to see her face to face.

In the meantime, of course, she had to keep doing her real job, while avoiding tripping any switches at Internal Affairs. She had a friend there, Kira Jones, a former Major Crimes detective, but Erin didn't know whether she could trust Kira to warn her of trouble upstairs.

If the NYPD got suspicious, her career was in jeopardy. She might be fired, or even prosecuted, depending on what happened. If the O'Malleys found out she wasn't really working for them, they'd probably try to kill her, and Carlyle, too, for good measure.

The bottom line was, if she didn't love Carlyle, she had to be out of her damn mind doing what she was doing with him. No matter how good the sex was.

She smiled to herself. The sex was good, no doubt about that. Great, even. But was it worth risking her life?

Tomorrow, she'd find out whether she could fool a bunch of violent, paranoid gangsters. That thought didn't help her get to sleep.

Chapter 4

Following a restless night, Erin and Rolf were the first members of the Major Crimes team to arrive at work. The top message in Erin's inbox was a notification that Norman Ridgeway's autopsy was done. The advantage of working Major Crimes was that their cases went to the front of the queue. Erin fortified herself with another cup of coffee. Then she and Rolf went down to the basement, into the domain of the Medical Examiner.

Sarah Levine didn't even look up as Erin and her dog entered her lab. The ME was peering at a sectioned piece of some human tissue or other, intent on her work.

"Morning," Erin said.

Levine blinked and stepped back from the microscope. "That's true," she said after consulting the clock over the door.

"You've got the Ridgeway results?" Erin prompted. Rolf stayed at her side, but his nostrils were twitching. The ME's lab had some of the most interesting smells in the whole precinct.

"Yes," Levine said. She picked up a folder and flipped it open. "Norman Ridgeway, age thirty-six. Male, Caucasian, seventy-two inches in height, weight one-ninety. Cause of death, cardiac arrest as a direct result of acute cyanide poisoning. I didn't need to do a full blood workup. Cyanide presents with obvious symptoms. The poison was ingested shortly before death."

"Was it the candy?" Erin asked.

"I've confirmed through stomach contents and dentition that the victim ingested at least one piece of chocolate at approximately the time of death," Levine said. "The absence of other food particles in the teeth suggests the chocolate was the medium by which the poison was introduced. Additionally, I tested the remaining chocolates in the assortment. One uneaten piece also tested positive for a lethal dosage of cyanide. Almond nougat, according to the label on the packaging."

"So, it's officially a homicide?"

Levine nodded. "Correct. Unless the victim knew the chocolates were poisoned, in which case it would be suicide, either assisted or solo."

"Anything else the autopsy told you?" Erin asked.

"The mouth swab turned up trace amounts of lipstick, coral pink in color. The same color of lipstick turns up in trace amounts elsewhere on the body, particularly on the—"

"I get the picture," Erin said quickly. She didn't need that image, especially with Ridgeways corpse lying right there beside them.

"The lipstick suggested that I could probably retrieve usable DNA from both the mouth swab and all other points of contact," Levine went on.

Erin nodded. Amber Hayward had been wearing coral pink lipstick, and it had looked a little smudged. "Is that it?" she asked.

"The victim was sexually active within the twenty-four hours preceding death."

"No shit," Erin said. "Tell me something I don't know."

"I'm referring to a prior encounter," Levine said. "I found some trace fluids. He'd showered between encounters, but some evidence was left behind."

"With the same woman?"

Levine shrugged. "I'll know when we run a DNA cross. If we had blood samples, we could compare blood types more quickly, but the encounter appears to have been insufficiently forceful to result in blood loss to either party. The DNA will be three months' turnaround, given the current lab backlog."

Erin wrinkled her nose at the other woman. "So, you're saying it's a bad thing he didn't like it rough?"

The Medical Examiner shrugged again. "The more violent the encounter, the more forensic evidence is likely to remain."

"It might be better not to describe it that way to the Lieutenant, if he ever comes down here."

"Voltaire said, 'To the living we owe respect, but to the dead we owe only the truth.'" Levine paused. "Of course, he said it in French."

Erin was startled. "You've read Voltaire?"

"Only the stuff he wrote about death."

*   *   *

Erin gladly retreated from the formaldehyde stench of Levine's laboratory, back to the Major Crimes office. Webb had gotten there while she'd been downstairs. He was frowning at their whiteboard, a cup of coffee in one hand, his customary unlit cigarette in the other.

"We need to know what Ridgeway was doing before he died," Erin said by way of greeting. "And who he was doing it with. I think we might have another suspect."

Webb raised his eyebrows. "Do tell."

"He was getting it on with the hygienist when he died," she said.

"Yeah, we know."

"According to Levine, he was doing something similar within the past day."

"The hygienist again?"

"Maybe. But she thinks maybe not."

Webb nodded thoughtfully. "Okay, we need to make sure. Get in touch with the Hayward girl, find out if she was the partner. If not, then we need to know who else was in the picture. If there's another girlfriend, and she's the jealous type, maybe she figured a way to poison him. Hell, maybe she thought she'd take out him and Hayward both."

"Or maybe Hayward's jealous herself," Erin added. "And she fed Ridgeway the chocolate."

Webb nodded. "You're right. Good work, Detective. Not even nine in the morning, and you've lengthened the suspect list by two. Maybe a little later, we can start whittling it down again."

Vic came out of the stairwell, holding a big soda cup. "Give me good news," he said. "I struck out with the Feds yesterday. They've got this firewall of petty bureaucrats in the RICO division. I wasn't able to get through to anyone important."

"Levine finished checking our victim, and the candy box," Erin said. "One of the other chocolates was poisoned. Almond flavored."

"Good," Vic said. "I don't like almonds."

"Hides the cyanide taste," Webb said. "Not that it'd do our victim any good. Your average Joe doesn't keep an antidote kit lying around."

"It makes sense not to poison all the candy," Erin said. "Especially if you want to throw off suspicion by eating with the victim."

"Risky," Vic said. "You ever try to track down your favorite flavor in one of those boxes? Get it turned around, you might get a mouthful of poison. Or worse, coconut shavings."

"That's worse?" she asked.

"Cyanide kills you," he replied. "You only wish coconut could."

"Sorry they don't make vodka-flavored chocolate," Erin said. "For your sake."

"Sure they do," Vic said. "You clearly don't shop at the right stores."

"This is all very interesting," Webb said. "But—"

"—we've got work to do," Erin and Vic chorused in unison.

Webb gave them a sour look. "Okay, we've got four suspects, currently. Rocky Nicoletti, Paulie Bianchi, Amber Hayward, and an unknown second girl. First order of business, we need to identify the Jane Doe. We'll start by doing a dump of Ridgeway's phone. It should be down in Evidence."

"I'll do it," Erin offered.

"I'll go after Bianchi," Vic said, a little too eagerly.

"No," Webb said flatly. "I told you yesterday, we have to move carefully with him. Rocky's still in a holding cell. I want you to lean on Nicoletti a little harder. My gut says he's not our guy, but he's the only one we've got right now. Shake him. See what falls out of his pockets."

Vic grinned. "One shaken loser, coming right up. What're you gonna be doing, sir?"

"Taking one for the team," Webb said. "Since you hate the FBI so much, and you couldn't manage to talk your way around a couple of useless desk jockeys, I'll get in touch with the Feebies. If I can convince them to give us the green light on Bianchi, that'll open up some options."

* * *

Erin checked Ridgeway's phone out of Evidence and took it
to the tech guys. These cops could break the encryption drug
lords used to lock their bank accounts; a Manhattan dentist
presented no obstacle at all. Their method, however, was a little
disturbing.

"He's got a biometric access," the techie told her. "We need
his password, or we just need his index finger."

"Can it still be attached to the body?"

He shrugged. "If you insist."

"I'm not bringing you a severed finger."

"Aw, man," he said. "I never get to do anything fun."

So Erin took the phone down to the morgue, and fifteen
seconds later, she had her access. The first thing she looked at
was text messages. She didn't find anything, which suggested
Ridgeway had deleted his texts. Back to tech support she went.

Retrieving the deleted files was almost as quick as
unlocking the phone. While they were at it, they disabled the
security and did a full data dump.

"This what you're looking for, Detective?" the techie asked.
He pointed to his computer monitor, where a sequence of flirty
texts from a number labeled "Vivian" marched down the screen.
They were interspersed with several to and from "Amber."

"Looks like it," Erin said, impressed and disgusted at the
way the dentist had been simultaneously juggling two
girlfriends' conversations. Some of the texts overlapped by mere
minutes. "I'll need everything off the phone."

"Sure thing," the other officer said. "I'll send you the package
in a few."

"Thanks." Erin took down Vivian's number and went back
upstairs. Webb was still talking with the Feds, or more
accurately, he was waiting on hold. She dialed Vivian's number
from her desk phone.

"Hello?" a female voice answered. She sounded cautious, and Erin didn't blame her. An unsolicited call from an unidentified number was most likely unwelcome.

"Hello, Vivian?" Erin guessed.

"Yes? Who is this?"

"My name's Detective O'Reilly, ma'am. I'm with the New York Police Department. I need to ask you a few questions."

"Is this some kind of joke?" Vivian retorted. Then she laughed. "Hold on, you're Monica, aren't you. Yeah, okay, good one. You got me. I believed you for a second."

"No, ma'am, this isn't a joke," Erin said. "What's your last name, please?"

"Hold on," Vivian said. "You're a cop, and you're calling me, but you don't know my name? How'd you get this number, anyway?"

"Norman Ridgeway," Erin said.

"Norman?" Vivian sounded surprised, then annoyed. "Geez, for real? He put the *cops* on me? What a jackass. And there I thought he was an okay guy. Look, it was his idea. I told him it was stupid."

Erin sat forward. "What'd he do?" she asked.

"I didn't even know it was illegal," Vivian said. "But maybe it is. If it is, it was his idea, like I said."

"Vivian," Erin said, leaning forward and speaking more urgently. "If you're mixed up in something, I can help you. But I need you to tell me what's going on."

"The restaurant," she said. "On Valentine's Day. We jumped the line."

"What restaurant?"

"Le Bernardin. On West 51st. Norm said we didn't need a reservation, we'd just wait for a name to be called that wasn't answered in the first ten seconds. Then he pretended to be the guy, and got us a table."

Erin sat back again in her chair, deflated. "He stole a guy's dinner reservation? *That's* what you're worried about?"

"Well, yeah," Vivian said. "But it's not like he took something for real. I mean, we paid for the meal. Why's a detective going after us for that, anyway? Don't you have, y'know, crimes to solve? Like, drug dealers or murderers or something?"

Maybe both, Erin thought. "I need to talk to you about Norman," she said. "What's your full name, please, ma'am?"

The other woman sighed audibly. "Vivian Berkley."

"Can you come in to the station?"

Vivian sighed again. "Do I have to?"

"It'd be a big help," Erin said. "But we can come to you if you'd rather."

"Okay," Vivian said, sounding like a pouty teenager agreeing to an unreasonable request. "Where are you?"

"Precinct 8," Erin said, giving the address. "When can you be here?"

Unexpectedly, Vivian giggled. "I'll tell Mom I'm helping with an important police investigation. She'll be pissed, but she can't say anything about it. I guess I can get there in an hour."

"Ms. Berkley, how old are you?"

"Nineteen."

Jesus, Erin thought. Norman Ridgeway had been a real piece of work. "I'll see you in an hour," she said. "Tell the sergeant at the front desk that you need to see Detective O'Reilly."

Webb was still on hold. He glanced at Erin as she hung up. "You got another suspect for us?"

"I don't think so."

"Why not?"

"She's nineteen. I don't see a teenage girl doing something like this. She sounded like she was practically in high school."

"Really?" Webb was unimpressed. "A teenage girl doesn't have the heart for revenge? Where'd *you* go to high school? She's on the list."

Erin sighed. "Yeah, she's on the list."

Chapter 5

Vic joined the other two detectives while they waited for Vivian to show up. The big Russian cracked his knuckles and smiled, leaning back in his chair.

"You're in a good mood," Erin said. "What'd you get out of Nicoletti?"

"Nothing much," he said. "I got a couple of his buyers. I'll kick it over to SNEU."

Erin knew all about the Street Narcotics Enforcement Unit. They were the notorious cowboys of the NYPD, running plainclothes operations against low-level drug dealers. She'd toyed with the idea of joining them, back when she was new on the force. Her dad had advised her not to.

"They're too close to the street," he'd said. *"All that cash, all those drugs, just lying around. Working plainclothes, doing buy-and-bust, getting too chummy with dealers and CIs. It's just a baby step from that to being a gangster yourself."*

Erin wondered what he'd say if he knew about her boyfriend. How the hell was she ever supposed to break the news?

"Why are you so happy, then?" she asked Vic, pushing her worries to the back of her mind. Drug buyers were a pretty low priority for the NYPD these days.

He shrugged. "Any day I can make a low-level perp cry isn't a day wasted. It beats the hell out of paperwork."

"You made him cry?"

"Only a little." Vic was still grinning. "I've dealt with hardcore criminals, and this Nicoletti's just a small-time punk. It's like if a Chihuahua was growling at Rolf, and we locked them in a room together."

"Chihuahuas can be nasty," Erin said. "They're more likely to bite you than pit bulls."

"But you're more likely to remember a bite from a pit bull," Vic retorted. "Trust me, this guy's a little yappy dog. Rolf takes on a Chihuahua, he'll eat everything but the bark."

Erin dropped a hand and scratched Rolf behind the ears. "You're not kidding. But he didn't confess to the poison?"

"Nope."

"Did he know his girl was sleeping with her boss?"

Vic snorted. "He says he didn't. But he did."

"How do you know?"

"He had to pretend. It'd make him less of a man otherwise."

"Little dogs want to look like big dogs," she agreed. "So he's still a suspect?"

"Yeah. And with him ratting out his dealer, the Narcs can hold him while we sort this out. When's this chick coming to see you?"

"An hour, give or take."

"Good," Webb broke in. "That'll give Neshenko time to fill out his DD-5 for Nicoletti."

"And just like that, the good feeling's gone," Erin said, smiling sweetly at Vic.

He winked and gave her an air-kiss.

Vivian Berkley swayed into the Major Crimes office on three-inch heels, wearing a tight sweater and a skirt a little too short for February in Manhattan. Her makeup and clothes were deliberately, self-consciously adult, but Erin, remembering their phone conversation, saw right through it. This was a kid playing grown-up.

"Miss Berkley?" Erin said, standing up.

Vivian gave her a bright, artificial smile. "That's me."

"I'm Detective O'Reilly. We can talk here, or we can go somewhere quieter."

The young woman glanced around the office with interest. "This is fine. Oh! You have a dog!"

"This is Rolf. He's a trained K-9."

Vivian carefully knelt to offer her hand to the Shepherd, tottering on her heels. Rolf gave the hand a polite sniff. "Can he smell, like, drugs and stuff?"

"He's trained in explosives detection, suspect tracking, and apprehension."

"Oh, yeah! I remember! You were the cop who did that thing at the Civic Center! They talked about you on the news!" Vivian's eyes sparkled. "Wait till I post this. I got to meet a celebrity!"

Erin made brief eye contact with Vic over Vivian's shoulder. He rolled his eyes at her, clearly trying not to laugh. He'd been right beside her and Rolf as the three of them had stopped a terrorist plot at the last possible moment, but no one was fawning over him. Maybe because he was just about the least photogenic member of the NYPD. Erin reminded herself to give him some crap about that later. For the moment, she'd leverage her fifteen minutes of fame to get what she needed.

"Miss Berkley, have a seat," she said, pulling a spare chair over to her desk. "Tell me about Norman Ridgeway."

"What about him?"

"What's the nature of your relationship with him?"

Vivian giggled. "It's not exactly a relationship. I mean, it's not like we're, you know, *exclusive* or anything."

"Is it physically intimate?"

"You mean, like, sex?" Vivian giggled again and glanced sidelong at Webb and Vic. Webb was ignoring the whole thing, pretending to do paperwork. Vic was watching the two women with an eyebrow sardonically raised.

"That's right," Erin said.

"Well, *duh!* What do you think?"

"You told me on the phone that you and Mr. Ridgeway had dinner together, night before last. Did you have an intimate encounter, either before or after dinner?"

"Both." Vivian giggled yet again. Erin was finding it more annoying each time.

"Did he give you anything as a Valentine's present?"

"Yeah. I'm wearing it right now."

"What is it?" Erin looked the woman over.

Vivian smiled slyly. "You can't see it from here," she whispered.

Erin didn't press for details. "Did you give him anything? Clothes, candy, anything like that?"

The young woman shook her head. "No, he buys me gifts. He says it's enough of a present that I'm there with him. Hey, what's going on here, anyway? Did Norman do something wrong? I mean, besides the reservation."

"We're trying to figure out what happened," Erin said.

"Is he under arrest?"

"No," she said truthfully.

"Is he in trouble?"

"Miss Berkley, do you know anyone who'd want to hurt him?"

"The guy whose reservation he swiped," she said with another giggle. Then she saw the look in Erin's eye and the giggle died away. "Wait a second. You're serious? Did someone hurt him? Is he okay?"

Erin kept looking at her, watching for any sign of a lie, any guilt. What she saw was a girl, younger than she wanted to be, a little scared and getting more scared by the second as the silence stretched out.

"Where is he?" Vivian asked. "How bad is he... what... how..."

"He's dead," Erin said. It was harsh, but detectives couldn't always play nice. She needed to see the girl's reaction.

"No, he's not," Vivian said. "I mean, I just had dinner with him two days ago. He had salmon... the organic salmon with... with peas and mint-tarragon sauce."

"Do you know Amber Hayward?" Erin asked.

The girl shook her head. "We had Tahitian vanilla ice cream for dessert," she went on. "At his place, afterward, he gave me champagne and strawberries, just like in *Pretty Woman*. He's not dead. You made a mistake."

Erin stifled a sigh. "Miss Berkley, I need you to think. Did you see a box of chocolate at Mr. Ridgeway's home?"

"Chocolate?" Vivian looked confused.

"One of those sampler boxes," Erin explained. "Like you get at a drugstore."

"Oh." Vivian's brow wrinkled. "No, I don't think so."

"Did you stay overnight?"

"Of course not! Mom would *kill* me!" Vivian paused awkwardly. "I mean, she'd be mad. She wouldn't actually kill me. Like, for real."

"Could you give me your address and your mother's phone number?" Erin asked. "In case we need to double-check anything."

"You don't have to tell her about Norman, do you?" Vivian asked. "Mom and Dad say he's *way* too old for me. You'd think I was still sixteen or something. They just don't get that I'm grown up now."

"Right," Erin said, noticing that the girl seemed almost as upset at her parents' view of her love life as she was at the news her boyfriend was dead. "If you could just write down that contact information, I think that'll do it for now."

"Okay." Vivian reached for the notepad on Erin's desk, then paused. "Hey, can I get, like, a selfie with you?"

Webb looked up from his paperwork and raised his eyebrows at Erin.

"Police don't give selfies during an ongoing investigation," Erin said with a straight face. She was pretty sure that wasn't in the Patrol Guide, but she was equally sure Vivian Berkley hadn't read the Patrol Guide.

*   *   *

"Well?" Webb asked, as the echoing click of Vivian's high heels died away in the stairwell. "Think she's a murderer?"

Erin shook her head. "I'm not seeing it. But I guess if she did want to kill him, it'd make sense to use poison. Maybe she wasn't trying to take him out, just get his attention."

"Like with suicide attempts," Webb said. Every cop who'd worked Patrol had been called to at least one scene where some unhappy girl had swallowed a bunch of pills. The victim often didn't really want to die. That made it all the more tragically pointless when they sometimes died anyway.

"If she gave him cyanide to get him to notice her, I'd hate to see what she'd do if she was pissed off," Vic said.

"We can't rule it out," Webb said. "O'Reilly, you worked that poisoning case last year, the Heartbreak Killer. Didn't he use the same poison?"

"Yeah," she said. "But that was a totally different MO. His scenes were always carefully staged. This? This is almost accidental. Anyone could've eaten those chocolates. Hell, the hygienist, Hayward, could've just as easily gone for an almond candy and it'd be her on a slab."

"That's what I don't like about it," Webb said. "Has it occurred to anyone else that the candy might've been doctored before it was even sold?"

Vic snapped his fingers. "Yeah. Like that asshole in Britain back in the Eighties. I forget his name. Rodney something-or-other. He was poisoning baby food on store shelves. Put some kids in the hospital. Didn't Reader's Digest do a story on him?"

"I didn't follow Reader's Digest growing up," Erin said. "But I remember hearing about that. My dad told us when they caught him. The thing I remember is, that guy was a former cop. That was how he kept ahead of the police for as long as he did. It was a blackmail attempt on the food company." She looked at Webb. "Sir, you don't think...?"

"It's a possibility," he said, looking unhappy. "If that's the case, we can expect some sort of demand for money, probably to the candy company."

"I can call them, see if they've gotten any blackmail letters," Vic suggested.

"If that's what's going on," Erin said, "we can expect another poisoning or two."

"I'm aware of that," Webb said.

"Do you have any idea how much chocolate gets sold in New York for Valentine's Day?" Vic asked rhetorically.

"We're not putting out a citywide warning," Webb said. "Not unless New York is prepared for a multi-million-dollar lawsuit from every candy company on the eastern seaboard, not to mention a general panic."

"What if someone else gets poisoned?" Erin replied.

"Then we inform the Captain, the Captain talks to the Commissioner, and the Commissioner takes it to the Mayor," Webb replied. "This shit rolls uphill. *Then* we have a panic."

"On the plus side, maybe it'll help New Yorkers with their diet programs," Vic said.

"I'll put out the word so we hear about any other cyanide poisonings," Webb said. "That's as far as we're going down that road. In the meantime, let's assume this was a personal killing. I want to dig into Ridgeway, find out what other skeletons he's got in his closet. This is the sort of guy who stole dinner reservations and juggled girlfriends. I don't care if he liked to talk dinosaurs with little boys. Let's face it, people were going to want to hurt him."

That was how Erin ended up spending her afternoon digging through a dead dentist's financial records. Not for the first time, she found herself missing Kira Jones and her knack for sifting data. It was like doing someone else's taxes, someone who didn't save receipts but insisted on itemizing everything. She found some little irregularities, but nothing damning. By the time they knocked off for the day, she had a dull, pounding headache. What she wanted was to go home, get a stiff drink, and crash in front of the TV. But she had a prior obligation. Carlyle was expecting her.

She had a little time to herself, at least. She took Rolf to the local park and did some detection training. She had training aids containing trace amounts of various explosives. She hid several fake items along with the real thing. Rolf unerringly detected the right sample, sitting in front of it and wagging his tail, but staying otherwise motionless. Erin rewarded him with his favorite chew-toy. Watching the K-9 happily gnawing, she felt a little better. Then it was time to shower, feed the dog and herself, and figure out what to wear.

Her closet was well-equipped for police work and athletics, somewhat less so for evening attire, and decidedly weak on gangster garb. She remembered Kira had worked as a gang task force liaison, and wondered if she should call up the other woman for fashion advice. Erin recognized this for the terrible idea it was. An Internal Affairs cop was one of the last people she should talk to on the subject.

The whole point was to sell the idea that she was head-over-heels for Carlyle. That meant she needed to dress for him, not for the others. Or, at least, to dress so the others *thought* she was dressing for Carlyle. With that in mind, she went over her wardrobe again and settled on a tight-fitting red blouse and figure-hugging slacks. She made sure to leave an extra button unfastened. Then, after doing her hair, she went to her cosmetics and picked out a more daring shade of red lipstick than she'd ever wear to work. By the time her makeup was done, it was half past seven. She'd have to go if she wanted to get there early, and she ought to touch base with Carlyle before the others arrived. Erin left her Glock behind, but she strapped her backup gun to her ankle, just in case.

"Be good, Rolf," she told him on her way to the door.

He gave her a look that could have meant, "Right back at you." Then he settled his chin on his paws, digging in for a long wait.

Chapter 6

Carlyle had suggested Erin use the Barley Corner's back door for this event, rather than coming in the front. It made sense; she didn't exactly what to advertise that she was meeting with the leadership of a major criminal organization. She walked up to the heavy steel door and waved at the security camera. After a few moments, the door was opened by a lean, tough-looking young man with a military-style buzz cut.

"Evening, ma'am," he said.

"Evening, Ian," she said, smiling at him. Ian Thompson, former Marine Scout Sniper, was one of Carlyle's most trusted guys. He'd helped her out of trouble on more than one occasion. He was the most polite man in the Irish Mob and, according to Carlyle, the most dangerous. If he was here, it was a good sign Carlyle was taking his security seriously tonight.

"Come on in," he said.

"I'm looking for your boss," she said, stepping into the back hallway. She could hear a faint buzz of loud conversation and cheering from the bar.

"First door on the left, ma'am." He pointed. His sport coat opened briefly, and she saw the Beretta tucked in his shoulder holster.

"Thanks." She walked past him and through the indicated door.

The Corner's back room was small, the round card table and chairs making it feel even smaller. A single light fixture in the center of the ceiling shone dimly through an amber lampshade. Two decks of cards and a box of poker chips lay on the green baize tabletop. Carlyle was the only person there.

He immediately stood when he saw her. "Erin, thanks for coming," he said.

She entered and closed the door behind her. "Didn't have a lot of choice," she said.

He smiled wryly. "I'm grateful all the same. You're looking well."

"You, too." He always looked sharp. His suits were well-tailored and expensive. The only time she'd seen him publicly disheveled, it'd taken a gunshot wound to make him lose his composure. "So, who's gonna be here?"

"The usual suspects," he said. "Don't tell me you've not read the files on the O'Malleys."

"Just what we've got at the Eightball."

"It'll be a fairly full house," Carlyle said, ticking off names on his fingers. "There's Evan O'Malley, naturally; your old friend Corky; Mickey Connor; Kyle Finnegan; Liam McIntyre; and two colleens, Veronica Blackburn and Maggie Callahan. Together with yourself and me, that makes nine."

"It'll be crowded," she said, glancing around the room. "What do I need to know?"

"You already know Corky and me. You needn't worry yourself about Maggie, she's harmless. And you needn't take particular notice of Liam or Veronica. Finnegan's all right, as long as you understand he's insane."

"Come again?"

"He was in a misunderstanding with a couple of UAW lads outside Detroit a few years back," Carlyle explained. "One of them put a tire iron into his skull. Finnegan was always a mite odd, and the blow scrambled him. You'd not know it most of the time, but it's best not to provoke the lad. Oh, and don't mention cats to him."

"Cats," Erin repeated, sure now that Carlyle was making a joke.

"Aye. He hates them." Carlyle wasn't smiling.

"Okay, don't pick a fight with the crazy cat-hating Irishman," she said. "Anything else?"

"Evan and Mickey are the ones to watch," he replied. "Evan's smart, he's sharp, and he's a right ruthless bastard. He has these get-togethers to keep an eye on the rest of us. Some of the folks in this room will be playing cards. For Evan, the game happens around the table, not on top of it. He'll not miss much, and if you make a mistake, he'll notice. Don't promise him anything you're not prepared to deliver, and don't lie to him if you can help it."

"And Mickey?"

"Mickey's a murderous thug," Carlyle said. "Most lads need a reason to kill. Mickey only needs a place. He's a former prizefighter. You'd think a lad his size would be slow. He's not. He's fast, he's strong, and he'd not think twice about hitting a woman."

"Nice friends you've got here," she said dryly.

He shook his head. "This isn't about friendship," he said. "It's a business meeting. Present company excepted, Corky's the only friend I'll have in this room. Any of the rest, except Maggie, would have me killed without a second thought. Most of them would do it themselves. On average, everyone in the room has killed more than once."

Erin took a deep breath. "Okay," she said with more confidence than she felt. "I don't suppose I could just arrest everyone in the room?"

He did smile then. "I don't think that would be wise."

*   *   *

The guests began to arrive a few minutes before eight. James Corcoran was the first through the door. He grinned when he saw Erin.

"You just cost me twenty dollars, love," he said.

"How'd I do that?"

"I bet Cars you'd not be caught dead with this sorry lot of gurriers."

"Corky," she said, "I don't even know what that word means."

"It's a bit of Irish slang," Carlyle explained. "It means a lad operating outside the law."

"Come, love," Corky said, walking around the table to sit on the other side of Erin from Carlyle. "Let's have a kiss."

She let him give her a quick peck on the cheek. He was the friendliest man in the Mob, a hopeless womanizer who'd only stopped trying to get her in bed when he'd learned she was involved with his best friend.

"How's business, Corky?" she asked.

"Oh, grand. Is this lad treating you right?"

She nodded. "He's a gentleman."

"Oh aye, that he is," Corky laughed. "But a gentleman's not always what a lass needs. If you're ever looking for a lad who's a bit livelier, promise you'll look me up."

"You'll be my first call," Erin said with a straight face.

The door opened again and a man and woman entered. Erin knew their faces. She'd told Carlyle the truth; she'd been through the O'Malley files at Precinct 8 beforehand. Liam McIntyre was a little guy with a face like a weasel and a few too many gold chains. He was a narcotics guy, and looked like he got high on his own supply. Veronica Blackburn was a tall blonde with the best body money could buy. She gave Erin a thin, challenging smile and guided Liam to a chair. She sat between him and Corky.

"Hello, Corks," Veronica said in a throaty purr. "I've been wondering when I'd see you again. You never call me back."

"Pressures of work, Vicky," Corky said. "You know how it is."

"Well, if you're looking to let off some of that pressure," she said, "I'm sure I can help you with that."

Up close, Erin saw the lines Veronica had tried to hide under the liberal application of cosmetics. According to her file, Veronica was forty-two, a former street hustler turned madam. To Erin's surprise, Corky seemed a little uncomfortable sitting next to the ex-hooker. He was being friendly, but with none of the flirtiness he usually deployed. Those two had a history.

Carlyle politely acknowledged Liam, who returned the nod and rubbed bloodshot eyes. Carlyle and Veronica scarcely exchanged a look.

The door swung open again, rebounding from the wall. Mickey Connor filled the doorway. Erin had always thought Vic Neshenko was a big guy who worked out a lot. Mickey had two inches and at least forty pounds on Vic. He was, quite simply, the most physically intimidating man Erin had ever seen. His face was heavy-jawed, scarred, unpleasant. He'd put on weight since his boxing days, but under the fat he was still light on his feet. She saw the muscles moving under his tight T-shirt and knew he was every bit as dangerous as Carlyle had said. His pale eyes scanned the room. When he saw Erin, his brows came down.

"So you're Carlyle's new pet," he said with a thick Brooklyn accent.

Erin bristled inwardly, but kept her face impassive. She wasn't here to pick a fight, particularly not with a man with fists the size of grapefruits.

"Watch yourself, Mickey," Corky said. "She's liable to bite."

Mickey snorted. "What's it to you, Corcoran? You tapping her, too?"

Corky put his hands on the tabletop. To Erin's surprise, she saw the tension in his arms and neck. When he spoke, though, he had the same free and easy manner she was accustomed to.

"Sorry to disappoint you, Mick. I know you thought I was saving myself for you."

"Just keep talking," Mickey said. "Every time I hear your voice, I look forward to shutting you up."

Corky smiled a cold, midwinter smile. "Any time you want dancing lessons, big fella, I'll clear my card for you."

Holy shit, Erin thought. Those two guys absolutely hated one another. She glanced at Carlyle to see how he was taking this. He was watching carefully, but saying nothing.

Mickey paused, considering the much smaller man opposite him. Then he shrugged, as if Corky wasn't worth the trouble, and sat down next to Liam. A few seconds later, the door opened once more and the last three guests came in. Maggie Callahan was a little, mousy woman who didn't make eye contact. She immediately sat down next to Carlyle, picked up a deck of cards, and started shuffling. Erin, taking Carlyle's advice, didn't pay much attention to her, though she was curious. Maggie was the only person in the room who didn't have a file with the NYPD.

But Erin didn't have time to worry about her. Kyle Finnegan and Evan O'Malley had come in together, and they demanded her attention. It would've been hard to put two more different men next to one another. Evan was the perfect image of an old-school gangster, from his fresh-shined black shoes to his neatly combed hair. He had eyes like chips of dark blue ice. Finnegan looked more like an out-of-work professor, a little unkempt with an unfocused expression.

"Evening, ladies, lads," Evan said. "Thank you for coming. I understand we've a new arrival among us."

"Aye," Carlyle said, standing and, indicating with a slight nod for Erin to follow suit. "This is Erin O'Reilly. You've all heard of her."

Everyone around the table except Maggie nodded.

"Excellent," Evan said. He didn't offer to shake hands, but nodded politely. He took his seat to Mickey's left. Finnegan took the final chair, between his employer and Maggie. Erin and Carlyle resumed their seats. "Are you a card player, Miss O'Reilly?" Evan asked.

Erin remembered what Carlyle had said. Evan's game had just begun. "I'm not much of a gambler," she said. "But I know how to play cards. What's the game?"

"Texas hold 'em," Maggie said, looking at the tabletop. She set the cards aside and started counting out piles of chips. "Two thousand dollars, fifty-dollar ante, bets and raises limited to fifty dollars." She passed out eight piles of chips. The other players reached into their pockets and produced rolls of bills. Carlyle's was double-thick.

At least she wasn't wagering her own money. It'd been Carlyle's crazy idea to have her here, so it was his cash on the line. That was some consolation, because Erin realized very quickly that she wasn't likely to be winning.

"Maggie, love," Corky said. "Deal me a pair of aces in the first hand. I'll thank you in my prayers."

Maggie didn't respond. Instead, she looked at Evan.

"Deal the cards," he said. "Let's play."

*   *   *

Erin knew how to play poker, but was no professional gambler. And this was no friendly game. Her police instincts were screaming at her that several of the people in the room were extremely dangerous, particularly Mickey Connor. He was the sort of guy a cop would never lose sight of, no matter how crowded the room. But she didn't want to stare at him. Besides, Evan O'Malley also needed her attention, and she was trying to keep track of everyone else at the same time. There was just no way to play skillful cards in this situation.

She bet conservatively, trying to take the measure of the other players. Carlyle and Evan played like pros, giving nothing away, staying calm, watching everyone else. Mickey played aggressively, trying to intimidate the other players with big raises. Corky was reckless, bluffing as if they were schoolkids playing for pennies, laughing off bad luck. Liam was nervous and twitchy, unpredictable, but with a tendency to fold. Veronica didn't seem to care what cards she was dealt; she was too busy playing the players. Corky started a couple of times, and Erin would've bet the other woman had done something to him under the table. Finnegan appeared distracted, almost unaware of what was going on. Carlyle occasionally had to quietly say, "It's your bet, Kyle," to call him back from wherever he'd gone in his head.

Caitlin, one of the Corner's waitresses, breezed in every few minutes to freshen drinks. The most popular beverage was Glen Docherty-Kinlochewe whiskey. Erin stuck to Guinness, figuring she'd better keep her head as clear as possible. Liam opted for something called a "death by chocolate," which appeared to be a bastardized milkshake, complete with whipped cream and a cherry on top. She noted that Evan only ordered one drink, and an hour in, it was still half full. Finnegan asked for mineral water, which led Corky to comment, "Lad, she asked if you wanted a *drink*."

"Liquor makes me fuzzy," Finnegan said.

"Like a cat?" Corky replied with a mischievous twinkle in his eye.

Carlyle shot his friend a sharp look. Erin, remembering what he'd said about Finnegan, tensed and wondered exactly to expect from a crazy mobster.

Finnegan's cheek twitched and his whole body jerked slightly sideways, like a man getting a mild electric shock. He looked down at the tabletop and rubbed his thumb against his fingertips.

"People say there's more than one way to skin a cat," he said quietly. "But it's all cosmetic. Really, when you get down to it, there's just the one way."

There was a brief, uncomfortable silence.

"My bet?" Finnegan said, blinking and looking around.

And the game went on.

After that first hour, Liam was out of chips and Veronica and Finnegan were running low. Erin, to her surprise, had more or less broken even. Corky and Carlyle were winning. Erin was even relaxing a little. Conversation was remarkably commonplace. Even crooks liked watching sports and talking politics. No illegal business was discussed.

Liam excused himself and sidled out of the room. He'd been getting edgier as his pile of chips had shrunk, and Erin figured he had a date with a dime bag of powder. The game went on without him.

It was the middle of a hand, a little after nine o'clock, when things got out of control.

The flop in the middle of the table showed the ace of clubs, five of spades, and three of diamonds. Erin's hand was garbage, a seven and eight, and she folded in the first round of betting. Veronica dropped out, too, and was watching Corky with an intensity that was making him nervous. The other players were still in.

"Hey, Cars," Mickey said. "Got a question for you."

"What is it you're wanting to know, Mickey?" Carlyle replied quietly.

"I was just wondering how you and the city kitty got acquainted."

Erin glanced at Finnegan, but he didn't seem aware of the second mention of felines.

Carlyle smiled thinly. "One of the advantages of being a publican is that one has the opportunity to meet people. She walked through my door one day, and we got to talking."

Mickey snorted. "I don't believe it."

"Are you questioning my truthfulness, or my memory?" Carlyle asked. "Regardless, my answer's what it was."

"You sure you're not leaving things out? Like, maybe she gave you a ride in the sow crate?"

Erin suppressed a flinch. She'd heard the term before. A sow crate was a police car driven by a female officer, and was not something you said to the cop's face. She did a quick mental tally and decided Mickey was on his fourth drink of the night. He might be a little buzzed, but a guy his size wouldn't be drunk enough on four shots of whiskey to have lost his self-control

"You know as well as I that I've never been arrested this side of the pond," Carlyle said, still calm and controlled. "Unlike yourself."

"Yeah, you're slick," Mickey said. "You're so slippery, I bet you don't even need to lube up before you get it on."

There was a momentary silence. Looking around the table, Erin saw several startled faces. Even Finnegan seemed to be paying attention now.

"Mickey," Carlyle said, and there was a definite edge to his voice. "You've crossed a line. I suggest you take a good, long step back."

"An apology to the lady's a good place to start," Corky added.

"Oh, sorry," Mickey said. "I didn't know any ladies was present."

Corky's habitual smile had vanished. "You bloody gobshite," he spat. "Your mum didn't teach you manners, so I guess I have to."

Carlyle put up a hand. "Easy, Corks. This isn't your affair."

Corky smiled again, but no one would have confused it with a friendly expression. "Is this a private fight, then? Because I'm perfectly willing to pitch in."

"Anytime, pencil-dick," Mickey growled. He levered himself to his feet.

Several things happened simultaneously. Carlyle and Evan both started to speak. Veronica settled back in her chair and licked her lips, an expression of anticipation on her face. Erin dropped a hand toward her ankle holster.

Corky moved faster than any of them. Erin knew he had incredible reflexes. She'd seen him snatch a falling beer-glass out of midair, and interrupt a bomb between trigger and detonation, so she should've been expecting it, but she still didn't see his hand move. One moment he was seated across the table from Mickey. The next instant, a knife was quivering in the green baize tabletop, the blade planted squarely between the third and fourth fingers of Mickey's right hand. Corky was standing now.

"Still fancy your chances, big fella?" Corky asked.

"Nice trick," Mickey said. He plucked the blade out of the table with his left hand. "Except now I've got your knife."

Corky chuckled. "You really think I only brought the one?"

"That's enough, Mr. Connor, Mr. Corcoran," Evan said quietly.

Mickey slipped his right hand into his pocket. His fingers curled around something. Erin tensed and got ready to pull her piece.

"I said, that's enough, both of you," Evan repeated, ice in his voice. "We're not having this."

Mickey scowled. "Sure," he grumbled and resumed his seat. Corky held out his hands in a gesture indicating he'd never wanted trouble.

"I apologize, Miss O'Reilly," Evan said. "Mr. Connor was out of line. He forgot his manners. It won't happen again, I'm certain."

Erin fought the urge to moisten her dry lips. She met Evan's eyes and saw no softness at all. It was purely practical considerations that had made him intervene. Otherwise, he'd have happily watched the two men kill each other.

"Thank you, sir," she said.

"And I'll be having my blade back," Corky said to Mickey.

Mickey looked down at his left hand. "You want your blade?" He took his other hand out of his pocket and wrapped his fingers around the blade. He flexed, without apparent effort. There was a sharp, metallic snapping sound. He tossed the blade, minus its handle, across the table. "There ya go."

"That's a thousand-dollar knife," Corky said, but he grinned while he said it. "I guess I've no choice now but to take all your chips by way of compensation. Fortunately, I'd already planned to do that. I think it's my bet, Maggie?"

Maggie hadn't participated in the confrontation at all. She gave Corky a slight nod, her eyes very large and alarmed.

"Then I'll raise the full fifty," Corky said.

And just like that, the game went on, as if nothing had happened. Erin took a gulp of her beer and wished she'd ordered something stronger. It looked like being a long evening.

* * *

Corky was true to his word. He buckled down to the serious business of cleaning out Mickey's chips. He did it methodically and competently, so much so that Erin wondered just how good a gambler the Irishman could be if he put his mind to it. Inside half an hour, Mickey's last chip went into the pot, which Corky won with three jacks. Mickey scowled, but didn't say anything. Apparently he'd decided not to pick any more fights that night. He didn't leave, but pushed his chair back against the wall and concentrated on drinking Carlyle's good top-shelf whiskey and glaring.

Erin's luck ran out soon after, most of her chips winding up as part of Finnegan's stack, or as collateral damage in Corky's crusade.

"I guess I'm out," she said ruefully.

"You put up a good show," Carlyle said with a smile. "My first game with these lads, I lost my shirt inside of an hour."

"I don't remember my first game," Corky said. "I'd rather a lot to drink, I suppose. Found myself riding the subway to Brooklyn with empty pockets and a sore head."

"He won," Carlyle said to Erin in an undertone. "And he was reasonably sober when he left the game. What he did after that, I've no idea."

Erin was actually glad to be out of the game. It let her watch the others more closely. She noticed something interesting. Evan O'Malley somehow managed to neither win nor lose big. His chip total hovered around the starting two thousand dollars, no matter what. He didn't even seem to be trying very hard. His cold blue eyes roved around the room, never resting very long on any single person, but she was sure he was aware of everything that was happening.

Mickey was watching Erin, and she didn't like it. She was used to being eyeballed by sleazy thugs. It came with wearing the shield and being a woman. But the way he was looking at her was more than simple male lust. She saw anger, bordering on hate. She could feel the man's barely-contained violence. She tried to keep acting the part of a lovestruck woman, paying most of her attention to Carlyle, but it was hard with that vicious presence on the other side of the table. What she really wanted to do was pull out her ankle gun and slap cuffs on him. If her handcuffs would even fit around those enormous wrists.

"I think that's enough for one night," Evan finally said at eleven. The game wasn't over; Veronica was hanging on to a couple hundred bucks, and Finnegan was basically broke. Evan had his starting two thousand, plus an extra fifty. Carlyle had more than doubled his stake, and Corky had everything else.

"Good night for you, Corks," Carlyle observed.

"Night's not over," Corky said with a grin. "We'll see if my luck lasts till morning."

The various O'Malleys were getting to their feet, putting on coats. Veronica leaned over and whispered something to Corky. Erin was just close enough to hear her.

"You still look lucky to me. If you're not too tired, you and I could go somewhere and... talk."

"Thanks, Vicky," he said. "But I'm afraid I've a prior engagement. I'm sure we'll run into each other again soon."

"I'll make sure of it," she said. Then she swayed out of the room in her stiletto heels. Corky shook his head and sighed.

"What's the problem?" Erin teased. "She seems like just your type."

Corky turned to her with apparent surprise. "You think so? I prefer to put in a bit of effort. Besides," he added in an undertone, "the woman's a man-eater. She's had me in her claws once. I had bruises after, and you don't want to know where."

Erin couldn't think of anything to say to that.

"Thank you, Maggie," Carlyle said to the dealer. "You've done a grand job, as always."

"You're welcome," she replied. Those were practically the only words she'd said the whole evening. She disappeared into a brown wool overcoat and took up position a little behind Evan. The O'Malley chieftain worked his way around the table to Erin. He extended his hand. It was clean and well-manicured, with a Notre Dame class ring on the fourth finger.

"It's been a pleasure meeting you, Miss O'Reilly," he said. "I look forward to our further acquaintance."

"Thanks," she said, shaking hands. His grip was firm. Their eyes locked for a moment. Erin had to steel herself not to look away. The icy force of the man's will hit her almost like a physical blow. This was the first time she'd been up close to the head of a major organized-crime family. This was no two-bit hoodlum.

"It's unusual to have a peace officer at one of these gatherings," he said. "I trust you've found your experience educational and rewarding."

"Educational," she agreed. "Not so rewarding. Your guys got all my cash."

Evan smiled and for an instant he looked almost human. "I wouldn't worry," he said. "I'm sure you'll come out ahead in the end, if you look to your interests. Good night, ma'am." He turned and left. Mickey went out just ahead of him, acting the part of a bodyguard. Finnegan and Maggie followed.

"I'll be on my way," Corky said. "I think I'll just stop in the pub and get one for the road."

"Caitlin gets off duty at midnight," Carlyle said.

"Is that so?" Corky pretended to be surprised. "I'll take that into consideration. I hope your luck improves, Erin." He winked at her and headed for the bar. Then it was just Carlyle and Erin in the room.

"Well, darling," he said. "What did you think of the lads?"

She took a long, deep breath and let it out, trying to relieve some of the tension knotting her shoulders.

"I don't know how you hang out with these guys," she said. "Jesus, I thought Mickey and Corky were gonna kill each other."

Carlyle nodded. "I'll have a word with Corks," he said. "He shouldn't have let himself be baited so easily. I fear he was trying to impress you."

"I don't need a white knight," she retorted.

"I know that, and so does he. It's a reflex for him. He's not even trying to get you in bed."

"Maybe not anymore," she said.

He chuckled. "Aye."

"Mickey's a real asshole."

Carlyle nodded again. "I can see why they made you a detective," he deadpanned.

Erin had to smile. "I can't believe he'd act like that in front of his boss, though."

"Really? I thought it was obvious."

"Obvious, huh? Enlighten me."

"He was doing exactly what Evan wanted him to," Carlyle said. "You're a K-9 officer, Erin. Surely you know an attack dog when you see one."

"Evan was using him to test me," she said. "Without committing himself."

"He was testing both of us," Carlyle said. "Evan likes to understand the weaknesses of the people around him. He was probing for your buttons, to see which ones he could push."

"Did Corky screw up the test?" she asked.

"Perhaps."

"Did I pass?"

"We'll know in a day or two."

"How will we know?"

"If no one tries to kill you, you've passed."

Erin looked sharply at him, looking for a hint he might be joking. He didn't seem to be.

"Jesus," she said again. "How do you live like this?"

"The same way everyone does," he said. "You'd be surprised what a lad can get used to. In a way, it's no different than growing up in Belfast during the Troubles. You never knew when some lad would take a shot at you, or perhaps throw a petrol bomb. It was good practice for the Life."

"I guess I should go home," she said. "And try to get some sleep. That's assuming no Irish hitmen are waiting for me."

"I'd not worry about it," he said. "I think Evan liked you."

"How can you tell?"

"I work with gamblers. Everyone has tells, even the best. And I've known Evan for years. He doesn't trust you, of course. I'm not certain Evan O'Malley trusts anyone on God's green Earth. But he invited you in the first place, and that's promising. Small steps, darling."

"This whole thing would be a lot easier if you'd just taken me home to meet your parents instead," she said.

"You're only saying that because you've not met my mum," Carlyle said.

"She's worse than a *mob boss?*"

He smiled. "Perhaps you'll have the chance to judge, one of these days."

Chapter 7

"You look like shit," Vic said.

"I had a late night," Erin replied. "What's your excuse?"

"You kidding? This is me on a *good* day."

"You expect me to believe that?"

"That I look good?"

"No. That you've ever had a good day."

He considered that for a moment. "You've got a point. So, what were you doing when you should've been getting your beauty sleep?"

"Hanging out with thugs and murderers."

Vic smiled. "Hey, you get to do that at work. Why waste your down time on it?"

"Because the sex is good."

He laughed. "Another good point. Except now you're expecting me to believe you're getting any action these days."

"More than you." Erin was quietly amused at telling the straight truth, knowing Vic wouldn't believe it. Carlyle was right about the best way to lie.

"You two ready to do some work?" Webb asked.

"Sure thing," Erin said. "What's going down?"

"I heard back from our Federal friends." His voice was drier than usual. "They let me know that they have no objection to an interview of New York City resident Lorenzo Bianchi, in New York City, by New York City detectives."

"Generous of them," Vic observed.

"He may be under sealed indictment, of course, but they didn't tell me that," Webb went on.

"That being what 'sealed' means," Vic added.

"Neshenko?"

"Yes, sir?"

"Shut up."

"You were saying, sir?" Erin prompted.

"But barring that, there's no open RICO investigation on him," Webb finished. "That means he's ours if we want him."

"Do we?" she asked. "It might be his son we're after."

"We'll go after them both," Webb said. "The kid's more likely to crack. Assuming he knows anything, of course. We mainly need to establish which hands the candy passed through on its way to Ridgeway. Anyone along the line could've tampered with it."

"This is why mom always told me to check the seals on food packaging," Vic said. "And to watch for razor blades in my Halloween candy."

"Neshenko?"

"Shutting up, sir."

"You really think they'll talk to us?" Erin asked. "I mean, these are Mob guys."

"We have to try," Webb sighed. "We don't have nearly enough for search warrants for these mopes. Either they talk or they don't. They'll probably lawyer up."

"Where are we going?" she asked.

"Tribeca, right on the edge of Little Italy. Penthouse apartment."

"Fancy. I shoulda worn my good necktie," Vic muttered.

Erin gave him a look. Vic only wore a tie as mandated by the department. His ties were, as a rule, forgettable.

"The good one doesn't have coffee stains," he explained.

*   *   *

They parked Erin's Charger and Vic's Taurus outside Bianchi's apartment. The neighborhood was posh and overpriced, just the sort of place for stockbrokers, CEOs, Mafia underbosses, and associated sociopaths. The detectives showed their shields to the doorman and took the elevator to the top floor.

"So, the kid lives here, too?" Vic asked. "What is he, twenty-five?"

"I think so," Webb said. "They've got basically the whole top floor. Plenty of room. And you know how Manhattan real estate goes. It's cheaper for him to stay at Mom and Dad's."

"How much is this guy's rent?" Vic wondered.

"More than we make in a year," Erin said.

At the door to the penthouse, Webb glanced at the other two. "I don't know this guy," he said. "But he'll know us. Bianchi's been dealing with cops since the two of you were in diapers. He's old-school. I'll take the lead, but if either of you see an opening, feel free to pitch in. You never know what'll crack him open." He reached for the doorbell and gave it a firm push.

After a short wait, they heard three bolts being drawn back. The door opened a couple of inches, showing the chain-lock still in place. A young man's face appeared in the gap.

"Yeah? Whaddaya want?" he demanded in classic New York style.

Webb held up his shield. "Lieutenant Webb, NYPD. Are you Paulie Bianchi?"

A woman's voice came from behind the kid, the sort of strident, demanding voice Erin remembered hearing a lot back in Queens. "Hey Paulie! Who's at the door?"

"Cops," he called back over his shoulder.

"What do they want?"

Paulie turned back to Webb. "Whaddaya want?" he asked again.

"We just have a few questions, for you and your father," Webb said. "Mind if we step inside?"

"Get lost, why don't you?"

Webb sighed. "I'd like to do this in a congenial manner."

"The hell you talking about?"

"He means he'd rather talk to you than have me do it," Vic said over Webb's shoulder.

Paulie looked him up and down. "Whoa, you're a big piece of meat, ain't ya? Juice much?"

Vic tilted his head. His muscular neck cracked audibly.

"Yeah, real tough guy, hiding behind your badge," Paulie sneered. "And your boss."

"The only hiding I'm seeing is you behind your door," Vic said. "And your mom's skirt."

"Eat me, dickwad."

"Look," Webb said, stepping between them. "This is just a formality. We just want to talk, and we'll be out of your hair in a few minutes."

"Forget about it. You ain't comin' in here without a warrant."

Webb sighed again. "Kid, are you seriously telling me you've got something lying around here, in front of your mother, that you don't want the police to see?"

"I ain't hidin' nothin'!"

"Paulie!" his mom called. "Quit yappin' and let 'em in. We're good, law-abiding citizens. We got nothin' to hide!"

Paulie, still grumbling, unfastened the chain lock and stepped sullenly out of the way. The detectives trooped into the apartment. Paulie blinked when he saw Rolf.

"Hey, lady, is he, like, your seeing-eye dog?"

"My eyes work fine," Erin said, smiling. "He's for when I need extra teeth."

Rolf looked Paulie over, unimpressed.

The living room of the apartment was furnished in thick, heavy carpet, dark red curtains, and mahogany furniture. The whole effect made Erin think of a half-assed homage to *The Godfather*. It was probably supposed to be serious, but the self-consciousness of it made her want to laugh. She thought of Carlyle's courtesy and confidence. It was no comparison.

Mrs. Bianchi levered herself off the leather couch. She was a very large woman, dressed in black, who'd probably been pretty twenty years ago. She was wearing too much jewelry and makeup.

"You the guy in charge?" she asked Webb.

"Yes, ma'am," he said.

"I figured. The girl's too pretty, the boy's got no neck, and the dog ain't giving the orders," she said. "So that leaves you."

"Is your husband home, Mrs. Bianchi?"

"He's in his study. What you want with him?"

"If you could have him come out here, please, we'd like to speak with all three of you," Webb said.

"Hey, Lorenzo!" she shouted in a voice that could crack glass. "Get your old Sicilian ass out here! We got company!"

Vic's eyebrows went up. He exchanged a look with Erin.

After a moment, an older Italian man came into the room. He was wearing a red silk bathrobe and holding a cigar.

"Nina, you don't have to shout all the time," he said in a weary voice. "I hear you fine."

"Lorenzo Bianchi?" Webb asked.

"Yes?"

"I'm Lieutenant Webb, NYPD Major Crimes. This is Detective O'Reilly and Detective Neshenko."

"I don't suppose you've come to arrest me?"

"Would you like me to?"

The Bianchi patriarch looked at him with sad, tired eyes. "Is it quiet in jail?"

"Not particularly."

Lorenzo sighed. "Then there's no point. Nina, get some coffee for our guests, would you?"

"What am I, your maid? Get it yourself," she retorted.

"You're killing me," he grumbled. "A piece at a time."

"I'll get it, Dad," Paulie said, surprising Erin. She hadn't thought he had a helpful bone in his body.

Lorenzo sank into an armchair. "Thanks, Paulie," he said. "At least youngsters got some respect. Now, Lieutenant, take a seat and tell me what I can do for you."

"If we could wait for Paulie to come back, that'd be best," Webb said, settling into the chair across from Lorenzo. Erin took the other end of the couch from Mrs. Bianchi. Rolf sat bolt upright beside the couch. Vic remained standing next to Webb's chair, arms crossed.

"Paulie?" A look of concern crossed Lorenzo's face. "What's Paulie got to do with anything?"

Webb acted like he hadn't heard. He sat perfectly still, watching the other man.

Erin had learned a lot from the way Webb questioned suspects. Sometimes the best thing to say was nothing at all. Let the other guy squirm a little, worry about what you knew. With weak-willed guys, that was sometimes all you needed to get them talking. What they said would clue you in to their state of mind, which could direct the interview.

Lorenzo Bianchi wasn't having any of it. After a minute or so, he nonchalantly picked up the sports page of the New York Times.

"So that's it?" Nina demanded. "You're just gonna sit there reading your paper? What the hell's goin' on here?"

"Spring training's off to a good start," Vic observed. "You like the Yankees' chances this year?"

Lorenzo glanced at him over the top of the paper. "Maybe. I'm not sure about the starting rotation. I don't know if Tanaka can make up for losing Pettitte. Plus, with Rivera gone, they may not be able to close."

"Yeah, retirement's a bitch," Vic said.

Lorenzo sighed. "Sometimes, you just get too old for the game. Then you gotta hang up the towel, before they bench you for good."

"You're gonna talk *baseball*?" Nina said. "With the *police*?"

"I like baseball," Lorenzo protested. "Bitch," he added in an undertone.

Paulie came back into the room with a tray of coffee cups, a pitcher of cream, and a sugar bowl. Erin took a cup and added a dash of cream. The kid sat down between Erin and his mom. He was twitchy and nervous.

"Relax, Paulie," Lorenzo said. "Nobody's getting arrested here."

"How you know that?" Paulie replied.

"This is a fishing trip," Lorenzo said, folding his paper carefully. "Though I don't know what they're hoping to catch. You must have something better to do than harass a retired Italian gentleman, Lieutenant."

"What line of work were you in, Mr. Bianchi?" Webb asked.

"Sanitation."

"That why they call you 'Sewer Pipe?'" Vic asked.

"Who's 'they?'" Lorenzo fired back.

"Your colleagues," Vic answered. "In your other job."

Lorenzo shook his head. "I honestly got no idea what you're talkin' about, Detective. I ran daily operations for a waste-collection service, but I been retired more than a decade."

"Garbage pays pretty well," Erin said, looking around the suite.

"I'm an American businessman," he said. "Lots of people look down on garbage, 'cause it's smelly. But that just means they gotta pay to haul it away. The more it stinks, the more they're willin' to pay. There's a lotta cash in garbage."

"Valentine's Day was a few days ago," Webb said.

Lorenzo blinked. "Not sure how you got from garbage to hearts and flowers, Lieutenant. I don't follow."

"Maybe he's thinking about his love life," Paulie snickered.

"You got a girl, Paulie?" Webb asked, turning his attention to the younger Bianchi as if noticing him for the first time.

"I got so many I can hardly keep 'em straight."

"That's because you hardly bother remembering the names of those tramps," Nina said. "I tell you once, I tell you a hundred times. You lie down with dogs, you get up with fleas."

Erin glanced involuntarily at Rolf, who stared intently back.

"You're pals with Rocky Nicoletti," Webb said. He was deliberately jumping topics, trying to keep Paulie off-balance.

"What's Rocky got to do with anything?" Paulie asked. He'd been nervous and belligerent. Now he just looked confused.

"You gave him something for Valentine's Day," Webb said.

"The hell I did!" Paulie snapped. "What you think I am? I just told you I got lots of girlfriends!"

"This is the twenty-first century, kid," Vic said. "No one cares if you got a boyfriend."

"I think you misunderstood," Webb said. "You gave him a spare box of chocolate, to give to his girlfriend."

"What if I did? It's just—"

"Paulie," Lorenzo said. His voice was quiet, but the steely undertone in it made Paulie swallow whatever he'd been about to say.

"Is there a problem, sir?" Webb asked.

"The problem is, you're tryin' to get my boy to admit to something," Lorenzo said. He was angry now, and his accent was slipping back into the street accent of his younger days. "When he ain't done nothin.' I seen it a hundred times before. Maybe there's a box of candy you found at some crime scene. Maybe there ain't no candy, you just want him to admit to a connection wit' some other guy who's in trouble. Maybe that guy wants to save himself, he makes up a story about my boy. Point is, guys like us talk to cops, we gotta be careful. Otherwise, we take a fall for somethin' we didn't do. I think maybe I oughta call my lawyer."

"No one's being accused of anything, Mr. Bianchi," Webb said. "I'm sorry for intruding. Thank you for the coffee." He stood up. "And thank you for your cooperation."

Outside, waiting for the elevator, Erin and Vic were both just about ready to explode. They went off simultaneously.

"What are you—" Vic began.

"I can't believe—" Erin said over him.

"One at a time," Webb said.

"Ladies first," Vic said. "Or Erin, in the absence of ladies."

"I can't believe we walked out of there," Erin said. "They knew something. Paulie was ready to spill!"

"And they were about to lawyer up," Webb said. "That was everything we were going to get with the old man present. We want to lean on Paulie, we have to get him alone. If I'd pressed him, Lorenzo would've called his lawyer. And believe me,

Lorenzo's lawyer is going to be well-connected and extremely well-versed in criminal statutes. Then the whole thing gets shut down, along with any chance of Paulie telling us anything more. Besides, he pretty much confirmed he gave the chocolates to Rocky."

"You think he poisoned them?" Erin asked.

"I don't know," Webb said thoughtfully. "If so, I'm surprised he was so ready to admit it. And I don't see the point, unless it's what passes for a friendly prank for these guys."

"You've really thought this through," Vic said.

"Wisdom comes with age and experience," Webb said.

"It takes the place of muscle tone and bladder control," Vic said to Erin.

"Laugh now," Webb said. "Live long enough, you won't think it's so funny."

Chapter 8

"It'd be easier to nail down a suspect if we knew who the intended victim was," Vic muttered. He and Erin were staring at the whiteboard in Major Crimes. They'd laid out a chain of custody for the deadly chocolate. It started at the Bianchi household, passing from Paulie to Rocky Nicoletti, then to Amber Hayward, and ending up in Norman Ridgeway's stomach.

"Makes the motive simpler," Erin agreed.

"Let's see if I've got this straight," Vic went on. "Hayward might've poisoned Ridgeway because he was screwing the Berkley chick. But Berkley had access to the candy beforehand, so she might've done it to take out Ridgeway, Hayward, or maybe both. Nicoletti gave the candy to Hayward, and he knew she was cheating on him, so maybe he wanted to kill her, or her boyfriend, or both. But he got the candy from Paulie Bianchi. Damned if I know why Bianchi would want to kill Nicoletti. Maybe he was skimming on the drugs he was dealing. Usually gangsters take care of that sort of thing with a gun or a knife, but who knows? And then there's the possibility the candy was already poisoned when Bianchi got his hands on it, in which case none of this makes a damn bit of difference."

"That's about it," she said. "I guess one of us better call the candy company."

"They'll have a whole file cabinet full of threatening letters," he gloomily predicted.

"You got a better idea?"

"No."

That was how Erin ended up spending her afternoon sorting through dozens of e-mails and scanned letters from deranged New Yorkers. The chocolate company rep was eager to help. He was almost pathetically glad to provide anything she needed. Erin got the feeling he was imagining banner headlines screaming about tainted sweets, leading to the company's stock going into free-fall and massive staff cuts, including himself. The only thing he asked in return was that the NYPD not issue any sort of public-health warning without talking to his office beforehand.

The letters were a blend of commonplace extortion attempts, health-food fixations, apocalyptic rants, and deeply weird psychotic manifestos. Erin learned, over the next few hours, that chocolate was to blame for global warming, acid rain, teenage acne, sexual impotence, and North Korea. She wasn't clear on the logic of that last one, but the writer was both well-educated and clinically insane, so his four-page, single-spaced typing was strangely compelling. Or maybe compellingly strange.

"Well?" Webb asked just before five.

"I don't know, sir," she said. "Once you weed out the crazies, there's a few that might be credible threats, but we may not even be able to trace them."

"If they're e-mails, I can put Computer Crimes on it," he said.

"I'll forward them to you," she said. "What a waste of a day."

"Every lead's a waste," Webb said. "Except the ones that solve the case. And we don't know which those are until we solve it."

Erin smiled. "You're right. I'm just tired, hungry, and cranky."

"Don't sweat it," Webb said. "I think this one will keep for a day or two. No need to pull overtime on it. I'd like to brace Paulie again, preferably without his dad in the picture, but a guy like that, I think I'll let him sweat. It's not like anyone else is going to die in the meantime. Go on, get out of here, you two. I'll stick around a while. You young people have lives to get back to."

"I'm actually dead," Vic said. "Still got a pulse, and some residual EKG activity, but it's fading fast."

"I suspected as much," Erin said. "It explains your report writing. See you tomorrow."

"That's optimistic of you," he said.

*   *   *

One of the advantages of not trying to hide her relationship from the Irish Mob was that Erin could go back to the Barley Corner, Carlyle's pub. She'd saved it from being blown up the previous year, which meant, according to the unwritten code of bar owners, that her drinks were on the house. She liked the atmosphere of the place. Sure, it was full of mob associates, but that was part of the charm. These folks might inhabit the dark side of Erin's world, but it was the same world and they understood one another. Plus, when you stripped away the outer layers, they were the same sort of blue-collar Irish guys she'd grown up with.

She spotted Carlyle right away, in his usual place at the bar. He saw her come in and gave her a nod and a smile. As she and Rolf slipped through the after-work crowd, she saw Corky at a corner table, chatting up Caitlin. None of the other players from the previous night were present.

"Evening, darling," Carlyle said, standing to welcome her. "Still protecting our fair city?"

"It's still standing, isn't it?"

"It should be," he said. "New York was built by Irishmen, after all."

"So was the *Titanic*," she said with a grin.

Carlyle winced. "That's downright unkind, especially to a Belfast lad."

She gave him a quick peck on the cheek. "Glad to see you, too."

"Hey, Erin," the bartender said.

"Hey, Danny."

"What'll you have?"

"Shot of Glen D, straight up, and a Guinness."

"On the way." Danny produced a shot glass and a beer glass and filled them.

"Are you wanting to talk business?" Carlyle asked after she'd downed her Scotch and started on her beer.

She shrugged. "Not much to tell. We got a murder with a victim, but too many motives and too many suspects."

He nodded. "Anything I can do to help, you've only to ask."

"I may need to know a little more about Sewer Pipe Bianchi."

"What about him?"

"Is he in the drug business?"

"To my knowledge, he's in no business at all at present. He's retired."

"Was he ever connected with the drug trade?"

Carlyle rubbed his chin thoughtfully. "I'd heard when he was running his trucks, he used to carry more than rubbish from time to time. But that would've been a good twenty years ago."

"And his son?"

"Paulie?"

"That's him." Erin was continually astonished at Carlyle's encyclopedic knowledge of underworld figures.

He made a dismissive wave of his hand. "He's strictly low-level, a petty earner. I can't imagine he'd be doing anything you'd be interested in."

"Even low-level guys commit murders," she said dryly. "Especially the low-level guys."

"I'd not heard he was involved in the muscle side of his family," Carlyle said. "Though anything's possible. Would you be wanting me to make inquiries?"

"If you can do it discreetly. We don't know for sure he's our guy."

"Have you known me to be anything but discreet?"

She nodded, conceding the point. Then she raised a hand to get Danny's attention again. He finished serving a couple of burly construction workers down the bar and hurried back.

"I think I'll grab dinner," she said. "How's Marian's Irish stew tonight?"

"Good as always," he said.

"Then give me that, and another Guinness with it."

"Grand choice for a cold February," Carlyle said. "Forgive me if I don't join you. I've an engagement later this evening, with my employer."

"Everything okay?"

"Oh aye, he just has some matters to discuss." Carlyle said it lightly, but Erin saw he was a little tense. She leaned closer and put a hand on his arm.

"You in trouble?"

He shook his head. "Not to my knowledge."

"But you're worried."

"Darling, anyone who goes to a meeting with Evan without being at least a trifle concerned ought to have his head examined."

Erin tried to shrug it off. Having a mobster for a boyfriend was helping her appreciate how hard it was for some guys to date a cop. It was a dangerous, stressful life, and it was never guaranteed that your loved one would come home at the end of a shift.

The stew, when it arrived, was exactly what she wanted. It was steaming hot, rich, and tasty, with fresh-baked oat rolls on the side. She dug in with pleasure. Rolf watched her eat, but didn't lay on the begging. He was a German Shepherd K-9, not a spoiled house-pet. While she ate, she and Carlyle chatted about the Yankees' prospects for the coming season. Mafia, Irish Mob, or NYPD, everyone in Erin's underworld liked baseball.

"Are you doing anything later?" he asked as she mopped up the last of her stew with her roll.

"I need to get Rolf home and fed," she said. "I could come back, if you're not too busy."

"The thing with Evan won't take all evening," he said. "Suppose you come calling at eight."

She smiled. "Grand," she said, mimicking his Irish accent.

At that moment, her phone buzzed in her pocket. "Damn it," she muttered and pulled it out. "O'Reilly."

"Webb," the Lieutenant said. "We've got a problem."

"What's up?"

"Bianchi's dead."

"Dead?" she echoed, astonished. Carlyle, beside her, gave her a sharp look. She signaled to him to wait.

"Yeah. I called Patrol right after you left and asked them to keep an eye on Bianchi's place. I got uniforms doing drive-bys on

Hayward and Nicoletti's places, too, figuring maybe we'd get lucky if someone was gunning for them. They got a call a few minutes ago, 911 from the penthouse. Poor bastard was eating his dinner and went face-down in the spaghetti."

"You sure Paulie's dead?"

"I'm not talking about Paulie," Webb said. "It's his old man, Lorenzo. First responder said it looks like a heart attack. He called me as soon as the EMTs arrived and took over CPR for him. They took him to the hospital, but I'm betting he's DOA."

Erin leaned against the bar. "Jesus," she said.

"Bit of a coincidence, don't you think?" Webb asked.

"We don't believe in coincidence," she said.

"My point exactly. Meet me at Bellevue Hospital."

"Yes, sir." Erin hung up.

"Rain check?" Carlyle asked quietly.

"Yeah. Sorry."

"You needn't apologize. I take it Sewer Pipe Bianchi's gone to the great dustheap in the sky?"

She nodded.

"Foul play?" he asked.

"We'll see," she said. "Don't wait up."

*　　*　　*

Erin had spent too much time in emergency rooms while working night shifts as a Patrol officer. She was very familiar with all the ways city life maimed, sickened, and killed people. Bellevue's ER was bustling with hospital staff, patients, and family members. She shot Webb a text from the First Avenue Atrium. He came out to meet her a few moments later.

"They lose him?" she asked.

He nodded. "Dead on arrival, like I thought. Cardiac arrest. Probably what's going to get me in another five, ten years." The

Lieutenant absentmindedly patted his breast pocket, where he kept his smokes.

"You could buy yourself another decade if you quit with the cancer sticks," she said.

Webb smiled. "Maybe, but it'd be ten years without nicotine. Not sure it'd be worth it. I'll take my chances."

"Where've they got Bianchi?"

"Basement. The morgue."

"Didn't waste any time, did they?"

"They needed the operating room. I talked to the trauma doc. Fellow by the name of O'Reilly. Any relation?"

"My brother. Was he the one who worked on Bianchi?"

"Yeah. He didn't bother cracking the chest. Like I said, DOA."

"If Sean couldn't save him, he couldn't be saved." Sean O'Reilly, Junior, was an experienced ER surgeon.

"I told him we might need to talk to him," Webb said. "Get a statement. He told me to put my statement where only my proctologist would be able to read it."

Erin smiled. "Sounds like Sean. I guess he was busy."

"Yeah, a couple GSWs came in while I was talking to him. Two punks who caught rounds in some stupid gang turf-fight. I think he was trying to get rid of me."

"And Bianchi's family?"

"I told them to wait. They've got some paperwork coming, the receipt for what he had on him and the medical certificate."

"Where's Vic?"

"He said he was halfway through his third vodka when I called him. I didn't want to have to slap him with a DUI when he showed up, so I told him to stay home. It's not a homicide, at least not yet. Just inconvenient."

"Do you want to talk to the family first, or check the body?" she asked, choosing not to mention the whiskey and two glasses of Guinness she'd drunk that evening.

"The corpse will keep," Webb said. "Besides, I want Levine to check him. We'll talk to the family while we wait for her."

"So, you don't think it was just a heart attack," Erin said, looking closely at her CO.

"I'm just covering all the bases."

*   *   *

Nina and Paulie Bianchi were in one of the chapels set upstairs from the emergency room. Paulie was dressed in street clothes, a leather jacket with metal chains, but at the moment, he looked more like a scared little boy than a tough punk. Nina looked a little less shell-shocked. Her jaw was firm and she was holding Paulie's hand in a tight grip.

"Mrs. Bianchi?" Webb said quietly.

"What the hell are you doin' here?" she snapped, recognizing him immediately. "Mary, mother of God, you even brought the dog with you. Don't you got anything better to do than keep harassing us? He's outta your jurisdiction now, with the good Lord, I hope."

"I'm sorry to bother you at a time like this," he said. "I just need to know if Lorenzo was acting unusual in any way, or if there was any sign of anything being wrong."

"I'll say!" she retorted. Her Brooklyn accent was growing even more pronounced with her growing outrage. "Sure, he was upset. The cops come round knockin' on his door, accusin' his son of God knows what. You probably set him off, poor guy. He was outta the life, you believe that? Course you don't. You lousy cops never believe in second chances. You're probably one of them goddamn Lutherans, don't even believe in confession. I tell you, Lorenzo died in a state of grace, and he's singin' with the angels right this minute." She pointed up at the ceiling. "God rest his soul."

"Did he complain about chest pains, numbness, anything like that?" Webb asked, ignoring most of what Nina had said.

"He was always complainin' about somethin.' He said he had heartburn."

"But he was eating spaghetti?" Erin said, remembering what Webb had told her. "With red sauce?"

"And sausage and peppers," Nina said. "What can I say? The man liked his food."

"Were you there, Paulie?" Webb asked, shifting his attention to the kid.

"Huh? Oh, yeah," Paulie said. He seemed only half-aware of what was going on.

"Did you notice anything out of the ordinary?"

"I haven't been home for dinner much," he muttered, staring at his shoes. "Mom said we were gonna have a family dinner, for once, and I should be there. Dad was eating, and then he got this weird look on his face, he grabbed his arm, and said something about getting his pills. His face went this funny color, almost gray, like. I got up and ran to the medicine cabinet."

"What meds are we talking about?" Erin asked gently.

"His heart medicine," Nina said. "Nitroglycerin. He's on propranolol for his blood pressure, too."

"I couldn't find it," Paulie said miserably. "He must've moved it somewhere, or maybe the prescription ran out. All I found was an empty bottle of his blood meds in the trash, and no nitro pills at all. I looked everywhere I could think of, but I couldn't find it. I just... couldn't." He looked up at the two detectives with tears shining in his eyes, and Erin found herself feeling sorry for this mobster wannabe. He was a kid who'd just lost his dad, and felt like he'd let him down.

"It's okay, kiddo," Erin said.

"I called 911," Paulie went on, almost choking on the words. "By the time the cops got there, he was already... I mean, he wasn't breathin' or nothing.' I wanted to do that thing they do in the movies, you know, where they pound on your chest, but I didn't know how. One of the cops did that, and the other one called an ambulance, and they brought him here. That's what happened."

Erin didn't say anything. She'd responded to calls like that more than once. This wasn't a Major Crimes issue, she thought; just an everyday, commonplace tragedy. Even mob guys could have heart attacks.

"Thank you for your time," Webb said. "My condolences for your loss." He tilted his head toward the stairs. Erin took the hint and followed him out of the chapel, Rolf trotting beside her.

Sarah Levine had arrived while they'd been talking to the family. By the time they got to the morgue, the ME had put on her gloves and was peering curiously at the late Lorenzo Bianchi. The ex-mobster lay on a slab, naked and pale. Despite his considerable bulk, there was something oddly pitiful and helpless about him.

"Evening, Doc," Webb said. "What've we got here?"

"Male, Mediterranean extraction, age around sixty-five," Levine said without looking up. "External indicators point to a cause of death of cardiac arrest, with underlying causes of obesity and habitual tobacco use."

"Get the bloodwork ASAP," Webb said. "We need to know if this was a homicide."

"Was he on any medications?"

"Pro... pro something or other," Webb said. He looked at Erin for support.

"Propranolol," she said. Her dad took it for the same reason Bianchi had. A combination of a stressful career and a little more weight than he ought to carry had left Sean O'Reilly, Senior, with a whole lot of cardiovascular red flags. "It's a beta blocker," she explained to Webb. "Pretty commonly prescribed."

"Correct," Levine said. "Anything else?"

"Nitro pills," Erin said.

Levine nodded. She took out a syringe and got ready to draw the first blood sample.

"Excuse me," said a voice from the doorway. It was polite and pleasantly smooth. Erin and Webb turned to see who it was. Levine, with her usual lack of social awareness, ignored the newcomer completely.

The man at the door was Italian, middle-aged, without a hint of gray in his slicked-back hair. He wore a very expensive suit, perfectly tailored. He smiled the most genuine fake smile Erin could remember seeing.

"I'm going to have to ask you to step away from the deceased gentleman, please," he said.

"On whose authority?" Webb asked. His own tone was polite enough, but he shifted his feet just a little, angling his body, and eased his right hand back, brushing the flap of his trench coat to clear his access to his revolver. Erin, taking the hint, took two steps to the side, opening the angle between her and the other detective. She didn't like the look of the guy. He was too polished, too deliberately polite. He was either a lawyer or a gangster, and in either case, she didn't trust him one bit.

"I have the medical certificate here," the man said, drawing it out of the inner pocket of his suit jacket. "And I have the family's request that the body be cremated. I'll be taking custody, effective immediately."

"And who, exactly, are you?" Webb asked. His tone wasn't so polite anymore.

"Vincenzo Moreno," he said, giving another of his full, earnest smiles. Erin reflected that he was very handsome in a dark, debonair way. It didn't make her trust him more. "I assure you, I have all the proper documents here. Feel free to inspect them." He handed the papers to Webb, who looked through them with a scowl.

"This is an official NYPD investigation," Erin said. "You can't just come in here..."

"Detective... O'Reilly, unless I'm mistaken?" Moreno said, turning to her with an elegantly raised eyebrow. "It is truly a pleasure, Detective. I've heard so very much about you. You're quite the celebrity in our city." He offered his hand.

She didn't shake it. Rolf interposed himself between his partner and the newcomer. His hackles rose on his neck. He could feel the tension between Erin and the stranger, and he was ready for trouble.

"Mr. Moreno," she said, "we're engaged in a homicide investigation. I'm sure you'll be able to claim Mr. Bianchi's remains as soon as we're done here. In the meantime, if you'd like to wait upstairs..."

Moreno's smile didn't falter. "I suggest you confer with your senior colleague, Detective," he said.

Webb was still scowling at the paper, as if he could ignite it with his eyes. "He's right," he said softly.

"What?" Erin demanded.

"The medical certificate states cardiac arrest as the official cause of death," Webb said. He met Moreno's eyes. "I would love to know how you convinced a doctor to sign off on this before the Medical Examiner had even shown up."

"That's not precisely the point, Detective," Moreno said. "I suppose the real question before us is whether you're prepared to honor the instructions in this lawfully-procured document. I'm sure you are. I'm certain none of us want any unpleasant confrontation. We're gentlemen here. Begging your pardon, Detective O'Reilly, Doctor."

Levine was watching Moreno with detached curiosity. Erin was staring at him, outraged. Every instinct told her this guy was dirty, that he was up to something, but she couldn't do a damn thing about it.

Webb drew in a slow, deep breath. His jaw worked as if he was chewing on his words before spitting them out.

"Have it your way, Mr. Moreno," he said. "Since the hospital's released the body into your possession, he's all yours. I'm sure you've got plenty of experience handling body removal."

"Excellent." If Moreno was bothered by Webb's obvious hostility, he gave no sign of it. He whistled sharply. Two burly guys immediately came into the room. They'd been waiting right outside. Their suits were cheaper than his, and they looked like they spent a lot of time at the gym. If they weren't Mob muscle, Erin would eat her own dress blues. At Moreno's direction, they wheeled in a gurney with an empty body bag. They shifted Lorenzo's body into the bag, zipped it closed, and rolled it out of the morgue to the elevator.

"Thank you, Detectives," Moreno said. "And thank you, also, for the very fine work you do for our city. Good day." He turned and followed his men out, his perfectly-shined shoes clicking on the hard floor.

Chapter 9

"Damn," Webb said. He said it quietly, almost meditatively.

"There goes our evidence," Erin said. She pulled out her phone. "I'll call Judge Ferris. If we get a court order, we can get the body back, at least for a little while."

"And we can see what we can distill from the ashes," Webb said. "Forget it, O'Reilly. Did that seem like the kind of guy who goes off half-cocked? His ducks were lined up in a neat little row before he came down here. They had the gurney, the body bag, everything ready to go. Twenty bucks says they've already got a guy at the funeral home with the crematorium fired up. It doesn't matter how fast we move, it won't be fast enough."

"So that's it?" Erin demanded.

"It may not matter," he said. "Maybe it was just a heart attack."

"Well, we'll never know now, will we!"

"Not right away," Levine said.

Both detectives turned to look at her. They'd momentarily forgotten she was there.

"Bloodwork takes time," she explained.

"With what blood, Doctor?" Webb asked.

"This blood." She pulled her syringe out of her evidence kit. It was filled with a liquid so dark red it looked purple.

"You took it while he was talking to us," Erin said, grinning.

"Of course," Levine said. "I wasn't involved in the conversation, so I was working."

"If I hadn't taken sensitivity training," Webb said, "I just might kiss you."

"Please don't," Levine said. "Secondhand smoke is a known carcinogen."

"Get that sample back to the lab and get to work on it," he said. "There's something in it this Moreno character didn't want us to find out about. I want to know what it is. O'Reilly, you and I have some investigating to do."

"Doing what, sir?"

"Family reunion."

"You want to talk to my brother," she said.

"I do."

*   *   *

"I can't talk right now."

Sean O'Reilly, Junior didn't bother looking at Webb and Erin. He was scrubbing his hands, getting ready to go into the operating room.

"This will just take a moment," Webb said.

"There's a sixteen-year-old kid in there with a bullet lodged in his spleen," Sean said, without pausing in his preparations. "They've just prepped him for surgery. He's bleeding out internally as we speak, and the spleen's a bitch to patch up. I don't have a moment. And Erin, you know you can't bring your dog into this place."

"Junior," Erin said. "C'mon. We just need to know one thing."

"Make it quick," he said on his way to the door. "And I'm serious. Don't get that mutt anywhere near my OR."

"Did you sign off on the medical certificate for Lorenzo Bianchi?" she asked.

That brought Sean up short. "What are you talking about? I haven't had time for the paperwork on a stiff. I was gonna go down to the morgue after I close this kid up and take care of it."

"Well, someone signed it," Webb said.

"What was the name?" Sean asked.

"It looked like a P followed by a loop and some squiggles," Webb said dryly. "The last letter might have been an 'I.'"

"You sure it was a doc?"

"Pretty sure. All you guys' handwriting looks the same."

Sean snorted. "Sounds like it could be Petrucelli. But he's a physical rehab guy. He wouldn't be signing medical certificates."

"Not in the normal course of things," Webb agreed. "Petrucelli, you say?"

"Yeah. Two Ls, ends with an I," Sean said. "Now I gotta get in there."

"Thanks, big bro," Erin said. "Go save a life."

"Don't end up on my table," he replied, giving her a quick smile. Then he was gone.

"Petrucelli," Erin said. "Italian name."

"That doesn't mean anything," Webb said. "Not by itself. But the coincidences are really starting to pile up. Follow me."

*   *   *

They found Doctor Petrucelli in his office, filling out paperwork. He was a little guy with wire-rimmed glasses and a reedy mustache that reminded Erin of Detective Spinelli, one of her old adversaries from her days working Patrol. He was scribbling what appeared to be complete gibberish on a hospital form.

"Doctor?" Webb said, knocking lightly on his door.

Petrucelli started in surprise, his pencil leaving a squiggle on the page. He adjusted his specs and blinked at them. "What's that creature doing in here?"

"I'm Lieutenant Webb, NYPD Major Crimes," Webb said. "This is Detective O'Reilly and her K-9."

"I don't know what I can do for the New York Police Department," he said. "I'm really quite busy this evening."

"I know," Webb said. "I saw some of your work just a few minutes ago." He'd gotten a copy of the medical certificate from the hospital files on the way up. Now he held up that piece of paper and leaned over Petrucelli's desk, comparing signatures. "Yes, this definitely appears to be your handwriting."

"Lieutenant, I really must ask you to leave," Petrucelli said. "If you have a court order, or some other sort of documentation, I'm sure we can accommodate any reasonable request. But for now, please be about your business and let me be about mine."

"Of course," Webb said, stepping back. "Good evening, sir."

Erin let them get a few yards down the hallway before asking, "What was the point of that? You just wanted to compare signatures?"

"And get a look at the guy," Webb said. "Obviously, he wasn't anywhere near the emergency room. He never saw Bianchi's body."

"And he filed a bogus report," Erin said. "Don't they take away your medical license for shit like that?"

Webb nodded. "I'm guessing Petrucelli's got protection," he said. "Unless we make a real stink, I don't think they'll follow through on any serious disciplinary action."

"We're pretty good at making a stink," Erin said.

Webb chuckled. "We are at that. But before you go to war, it's a good idea to know what your objectives are. Right now, Petrucelli doesn't matter. He's just a name on a piece of paper. But Moreno... that's a guy worth looking into."

"I'll get on it, sir."

He smiled wryly. "Okay. See what you can find out from your sources. Neshenko and I will check the files at the Eightball. This guy's going to have a record, I'd bet my shield on it."

So Erin found herself heading back to the Barley Corner after all, but with a different purpose in mind.

*　　*　　*

It was middle evening when Erin walked into the Corner for the second time that night. The place was even busier than before. The big-screen TVs were showing the Winter Olympics, and Erin knew a lot of money was changing hands on the outcome of the events. A crowd of raucous guys was cheering the women's alpine skiers. She suspected the cheers had as much to do with the women as with the competition.

Carlyle was nowhere in sight. She paused, looking around the place. Rolf stuck close to her side. He was used to the Corner, but he sensed his partner's hesitation.

"Erin, love! Over here!"

"Corky," she said under her breath. He was at a booth by the window, accompanied by a pair of burly, scruffy-looking guys. James Corcoran waved her over.

She crossed the room. Corky stood up and made room for her next to him. The other two, less gentlemanly, remained seated and gave her an appreciative look.

"Lads, this is Erin O'Reilly," he said, extending an arm. "She's in with the toughest gang in the city, the boys in blue. Erin, this is Pat and Goat."

"Pleased to meet you, boys," Erin said. She sat down beside Corky, making sure to keep his hands in view. You never could tell with him.

"Well, aren't you a fine ride," Goat said with a grin and an Irish accent even thicker than Corky's. "It's a pleasure to meet you, lass. You're a right feek and no mistake."

Erin blinked. "Excuse me?"

"Cop on, lad," Corky said. "Stop being a bloody gobshite." To Erin, he added, "He's a jackeen just over from the old country. Even I can't understand him half the time. If he gives you trouble, just puck him one in the gob."

"Corky," she replied, "I don't know half the words you just used either."

He grinned. "It's talking to these lads from back home gets me that way. A jackeen's a fellow from Dublin."

"So, you're one of the Garda, like?" Goat asked. "I tell you, Corks, even the coppers are prettier over here. I bloody love America."

Pat was looking at Rolf with interest. He offered his hand. Rolf, unimpressed, gave him a cursory sniff and a cool look. The Shepherd settled at Erin's feet.

"Guinness, love, or something harder?" Corky asked.

"Guinness," she said. Corky signaled Caitlin, holding up four fingers. Four pints of stout quickly appeared.

"So, what do you lads do?" Erin asked, taking a sip of her drink.

"Dockyards," Goat said. "Loading the great ships, love. Me and my sham here," he elbowed Pat, "we're just over on a visit, seeing where the ships come in. Seems they all come to New

York. Say, you sure you're a Guard? You're a right deadly beour, and I could stall you for bloody hours."

"Goat," Corky said, "those lines don't even work on a lass who knows what the devil you're talking about. Over here, you've no chance at all. Give it up, lad. You're embarrassing yourself. Besides, she's spoken for."

"American colleens like a bit of Irish," Goat protested.

Corky smiled. "Well, Erin? Do you like Goat?"

She gave it a minute, playing along, looking him over. Then she cocked an eyebrow and shook her head. Goat wiped away an imaginary tear and took a big gulp of Guinness.

"Carlyle isn't back yet?" Erin asked Corky.

He shook his head. "He should be here soon. Something you're needing him for?"

"I ran into a guy earlier this evening, thought he might know him."

"Who was he?" Corky asked.

"An Italian. Called himself Vincenzo Moreno."

"Oh, that'd be Vinnie the Oil Man," Corky said, nodding.

"You know him?"

"Aye, we've run into each other time and again."

"How big a fish is he?"

"You don't worry about the size of the fish," Corky said. "You worry about the size of its teeth. The blue whale's the biggest bloody fish in the ocean, but it's got no teeth at all and lives on wee shrimps and suchlike."

"A whale's not a fish, Corky," she said.

He waved her objection away. "That's not the point. Vinnie's no fish either. He's a squid."

"Corky?"

"Aye, love?"

"How drunk are you?"

He gave her a charmingly lopsided smile. "I'll be much drunker later."

"How is Vinnie like a squid?"

"You know how they squirt a great cloud of ink on you when you scare them?"

"Yeah?"

"He's like that. He's all smooth manners and handshakes, then next thing you know, you're left with nothing but a black, slimy cloud in the water and he's gone. That's why they call him the Oil Man. He's slippery like you'd not believe."

"Who's he work for?"

"Acerbo."

Erin recognized the name immediately. Vittorio Acerbo was head of the Lucarelli Family, one of the notorious Mafia clans of New York. Acerbo was in prison, had been for two solid decades, but was still nominally in charge of the family. "You mean he works directly for Acerbo, or are there layers?"

Corky shrugged. "You'd have to ask the Italians, love. But we're not here for business tonight, Erin. I'm here to watch young lasses in skintight Spandex swing their hips on their way down the ski slopes."

"You're incorrigible."

He grinned. "I hope so." He slipped a hand under the table and squeezed her leg just above the knee.

Erin slapped his hand away. He didn't mean anything by it. He'd stopped actively trying to seduce her when she'd gotten involved with Carlyle. Now it was just a game, and she knew the rules as well as he did. It was plain Corky didn't want to talk more about the underworld, particularly in front of the two Irishmen, who were almost certainly smuggling contacts of the O'Malleys. She settled back and watched the skiing instead, trying not to be too impatient.

She was doing her best not to worry about Carlyle, but her heart jumped every time the door opened. Customers came and went. Time passed. She chatted with Corky and his two colleagues about things that didn't matter. She had a second Guinness.

The door opened yet again, and Carlyle came in. He made his way to the bar, smiling at everyone, clapping a few of his lads on the shoulder as he went, but he looked tired to Erin. She saw the lines around his eyes and the rigidity in his posture. Whatever he'd been talking to O'Malley about, it hadn't been an easy conversation.

"There's your lad," Corky said. "It's been a rare treat, love. Do try to enjoy the rest of your evening." He winked.

"I'll do that," she said, standing up. "Don't get in more trouble than usual."

"No promises."

Carlyle had already seen Erin. He gave her a small nod. If he was surprised to see her there, he didn't show it. As she approached, Danny handed him a glass of Guinness. He took about a third of it down in a long, steady drink.

"Rough night?" she asked in an undertone, leaning her elbows on the bar beside him. Rolf padded over and sat squarely between them.

"Better than some," he replied.

"There's something I need to talk to you about."

He looked at her. "Ought I to be worrying?"

"I don't think so. I just need to pick your brain."

"Very well. I'm at your disposal."

"Vincenzo Moreno. Vinnie the Oil Man."

Carlyle glanced around the bar. Erin reflected, not for the first time, on the strange privacy of being in a noisy, semi-public place. There was so much background noise, between the television and all the side conversations, that they could be discussing just about anything without fear of being overheard.

"He's a colleague of Lorenzo Bianchi," he said. "But you know that already, I've no doubt."

"And they're with the Lucarellis," she added.

"Aye," he agreed. "And with the family boss incarcerated, thanks to your lot, the Oil Man runs their business in Manhattan."

"Really?" Erin was surprised a guy so high up the ladder would get involved with street-level operations.

"Aye," Carlyle said again. He drained half of what was left in his glass. "He's a dangerous lad. I can tell you a great deal you'll already find in your files, but suffice to say, he's likely second-in-command of his organization."

"What's he doing messing around the morgue?" she wondered aloud.

"You met him?" Carlyle asked. "Face to face?"

"Yeah. Smooth-talking son of a bitch. Good-looking guy, but uses too much hair gel."

"Aye, that sounds like him. What did he want?"

"He collected Bianchi's body. Probably so we couldn't run forensics."

"You're not the only one thinking Sewer Pipe might have been murdered, it seems."

She nodded. "Would he have a reason to take Bianchi out?"

"There's always a reason if you look for it."

Erin glanced sharply at him. "Was there trouble?" she asked in a lower voice. "At your meeting?"

Carlyle shook his head. "He wanted to discuss the altercation between Corky and Mickey at the game. I think he was primarily concerned that I keep a tight leash on Corks. Evan doesn't want the two of them at one another's throats."

"Why does Corky hate Mickey so much?"

He shrugged. "They've very different philosophies of life. Corky's a happy-go-lucky type, as you're well aware. He's never happier than when everyone's having a grand time of it. Mickey's the sort of lad who gets his pleasure from inflicting pain. If he's happy, it's a fair bet no one else in the room is."

"He's a sadist, you mean?"

"Oh, aye. Steer clear of him, Erin." Carlyle's face was deadly serious. "He's not a safe lad to be around, no matter what. This isn't admissible in court, but I'll tell you, he's personally ended more lives than everyone else who was in that room, put together. I've reason to believe he's killed at least one woman, a girl Corky was interested in. Corky knows it, too. And to my knowledge, Mickey's never used a gun to kill."

"What does he use?"

He hesitated. She was coming right up against the line they kept to separate her work from his.

"Come on," she said. "This bastard ever comes after me, I'm gonna need to know."

"His hands," Carlyle said.

"His bare hands? You're shitting me. So, what, he strangles them?"

He shook his head. "He carries twenty dollars at all times."

"I don't get it."

"Two rolls of quarters, one in each pocket."

Then she did understand. "Fist loads," she said. Some street fighters liked to use a roll of coins, clenched in the hand, to add extra weight to a punch.

"More legal than brass knuckles, and less suspicious," he said.

"Nice guy," she said.

"But we were discussing Mr. Moreno," Carlyle said. "From the sound of it, he doesn't want a thorough police investigation into Bianchi's death. Do you know what he's doing with the body?"

"Cremation, probably."

He nodded. "Stands to reason. That'll neatly dispose of most of the evidence. Are you investigating his death now?"

"We are. It's pretty suspicious."

"I'll be glad to assist." He smiled wearily. "Anything that causes mischief for the Italians will only make us look better in Evan's eyes. And he is watching, Erin."

She returned the smile. "You know, there's plenty of girls nervous about getting along with their man's family, but you take the damn cake." She looked him over again. "You look tired."

"I'm a trifle worn, darling."

"Then I'll get out of your hair. I'll see you soon."

"Take care of yourself, Erin."

"Back at you."

Chapter 10

Despite her run-in with the Mafia, her worries about the O'Malleys, and the accumulating bodies on their case, Erin slept well and woke up refreshed. She'd been feeling better ever since she and Carlyle had gotten together. There were any number of reasons for it, but she figured it mostly boiled down to not feeling alone. It felt so damn *good* to have someone who understood her, someone she could talk to about *anything*. It was completely crazy that the guy in question was a gangster, but that didn't bother her as much as she knew it should.

After her early-morning run with Rolf, she grabbed a croissant from a bakery on her way in to the precinct. Not for the first time, she blessed the coffee machine in the Major Crimes office. It'd been an anonymous gift, but it was an open secret on her team that it'd come from Carlyle, a thank-you for protecting his establishment. Erin poured herself a cup and sat down at her desk. Webb and Vic weren't in yet, and the place was quiet.

The first thing she saw on her computer was a message from Levine. Lorenzo Bianchi's bloodwork was done. She bounced right back out of her chair and hurried downstairs to the morgue.

Levine was staring at her computer screen. She was wearing the same clothes as the previous evening. She didn't look up.

"Morning," Erin said. "Did you go home last night?"

"No point," Levine said. "The bloodwork took most of the night. I took the blood sample from the heart. Ideally, I would have liked to have samples from various parts of the body, since drugs have different concentrations in different organs and tissues, but I only had time to collect the one sample. Urine would have been useful as well, along with tissue samples from the liver, kidneys, and vitreous humor. It only takes fifteen minutes to get all the samples. It would have been convenient if the man last night had been willing to wait for me to collect all of them."

"I think that was the point," Erin said. "He didn't want you to have any samples at all. But I'm surprised you're done already."

"I'm a qualified toxicologist," Levine reminded her. "That means I didn't have to outsource the testing. I have a two-week backlog, but Lieutenant Webb said this one was a priority. The lack of sample diversity is a problem, but it also reduced processing time. I hope you aren't expecting this rapid a turnaround on all samples. Four to six weeks is standard."

"Yeah, I know." That was yet another thing TV shows got wrong about detective work. "But you have answers?"

"Preliminary," Levine said. "I would appreciate confirmation from an independent toxicologist, and further analysis of the blood sample. That will take—"

"—four to six weeks," Erin finished for her.

"Correct."

"You'd better give me the preliminary report, then."

"Cardiac arrest," Levine said, handing her a sheaf of papers.

Erin glanced down at them. She understood maybe two-thirds of the words on the first page.

"What caused the heart attack?"

"The only foreign substance in the deceased's blood was a significant concentration of propranolol," Levine said.

"His blood-pressure medication," Erin said. "We knew about that."

"It was a significant concentration," Levine repeated. "Propranolol can cause cardiac arrest in sufficient quantity."

"You saying he overdosed on his heart meds?"

"That is my preliminary conclusion," Levine said. "However, his weight and tobacco use were both significant risk factors for heart disease. It's possible the cardiac event was unrelated to the medication."

"But you don't think so?"

"I have approximately eighty-five percent confidence the event was triggered by propranolol."

"Not cyanide?"

Levine gave her a funny look. "The deceased's symptoms were not at all consistent with cyanide poisoning."

"Or any other kind of poison?"

"As I said, I'm eighty-five percent certain—"

"Propranolol is a medicine, not a poison."

"That's an academic distinction," Levine said. "Many poisons can serve as medicines in the proper dosage and situation, and vice versa."

Erin nodded. "It's all drugs, I guess. But you didn't find anything else?"

"No."

"Okay, thanks."

* * *

Vic had arrived while Erin had been downstairs. He was drinking Mountain Dew out of an enormous plastic cup and glaring at the whiteboard.

"Morning, Sunshine," he said when he saw her. "You teach Rolf to like coffee yet?"

"Caffeine is poisonous to dogs," she said, thinking of what Levine had said about poison and medicine.

He looked surprised. "Really? Man, take me off the stuff and I'd eat my gun, if I ever found the energy to pull the trigger. How's that poor mutt manage to keep on living? Anyway, what've you got there?"

"Bloodwork."

"What'd Sewer Pipe have in his pipes?"

"Just his heart meds."

"So, not poisoned."

"Actually, maybe he was." Erin explained what Levine told her. Vic frowned.

"You think he offed himself?" he asked. "By accident, or maybe on purpose?"

"He didn't seem suicidal to me," Erin said. "I guess an accidental overdose is possible. Any idea how long he was on the meds? Maybe if he wasn't used to them, he just took too many."

"Nope," Vic said. "And good luck getting a court order for his pharmacist. If we even knew who was filling his prescriptions. I wish I'd taken a look through his bathroom trash. The bottle would've had the date on it."

Erin snapped her fingers. "Right! Paulie said he found an empty bottle in the trash."

"So?" Vic asked.

"So who throws away their prescription bottle before getting it refilled?" Erin asked. "If my dad runs short of his pills, he sets the empty bottle out as a reminder."

"I must not be awake yet," he said. "I don't follow."

"Whoever emptied that bottle didn't intend it to be refilled," she said.

"You think someone got rid of his pills?"

"Looks that way."

"But you said he overdosed, not that he ran out. What'd they do, hold him down and force-feed him? I can think of fifteen easier ways to kill a guy."

"What if they put the pills in something else?" Erin replied. She sat down at her desk and brought up her web browser. She looked up propranolol, specifically its flavor. "It's got a strong taste. Bitter."

"So whatever it was in would have to be pretty strong-tasting itself," Vic said. "Like, I dunno, maybe spicy pasta sauce? With peppers?"

Erin grinned at him. "Damn right."

"I like it," Vic said. "Of course, that would mean it was either the wife or the son who poisoned him."

"My money's on the wife," Erin said.

"Yeah," he agreed. "She'd have had an easier time slipping it into the food. Plus, she planned the meal. There's just one problem. You know what the Lieutenant would say about this."

"It's thin," Erin said, using one of Webb's favorite words. "Circumstantial evidence, jumping to conclusions. We don't have proof."

"But if she did..." Vic said.

"Then she might've tried once before," Erin said. "Like, say, with a box of candy?"

"Yeah," he agreed. "Unfortunately, I don't think we can tie that to her, either."

"But we should definitely look closer at her," Erin said. "Maybe find a motive, a receipt for rat poison and candy at the local drugstore, I don't know. Something may turn up."

"I always wanted to investigate the Mafia," Vic said. "But I never thought their girls were loudmouth bitches from Long Island."

"You got a problem with loudmouth bitches from Long Island?" Erin retorted, giving it her best Queens inflection.

"No," he said, grinning. "They grow on you."

*   *   *

Lots of spouses killed each other. Something like half of all women who were murdered were done in by a romantic partner. Crimes of passion, trying to collect life insurance, wanting to clear the way for a new lover, or any number of stupid reasons were enough. Some people even did it just to avoid the hassle of divorce court. But there was always a reason, however trivial. And the most common reasons were sex and money.

They couldn't find out much about the Bianchis' love life, but they could look into the household's finances. Erin and Vic started slogging through the dead man's files without much hope. Lorenzo was retired Mafia. After Al Capone had gone down for income tax evasion, the Mob had wised up and gotten good at laundering money. Accordingly, when Lieutenant Webb arrived, they had nothing to show for their labor. The visible part of the Bianchis' finances was completely innocuous.

"Interesting theory," he said when they explained what Levine had said. "You thinking the wife tried to poison him with the chocolate, failed, and tried again with his medication?"

"Why not?" Erin replied.

"Why'd she want to kill him?" Webb asked.

"Besides the obvious?" Vic interjected.

"Enlighten me," Webb said.

"You were there," Vic said. "Those two hated each other. It was just bitch, bitch, bitch the whole time."

"Reminded me of my second marriage," Webb said. "But I didn't kill my wife."

"You're not in a Mafia family," Erin said.

"If you're right, and the food was poisoned, there's only one way to prove it," he said.

"We gotta get our hands on the dishes," Vic said.

"She'll have washed them by now," Erin said.

"And we'd need a warrant to retrieve them anyway," Webb sighed. "Which we won't get. It was a thought."

"I'm wondering something, sir," Erin said.

"I'm listening," Webb said.

"If this was a marital thing, a personal murder, then where's Vinnie the Oil Man in all this?"

"Vinnie the who?" Vic asked.

"Moreno," Webb said, nodding. "Did your CIs give you anything useful on him?"

"He's a big player in the Lucarelli family," Erin said. "According to a couple guys I talked to, he basically runs things for them in Manhattan, since their old man's in jail."

"It doesn't make sense," Vic said. "Big guys don't usually sweat the small shit. He shouldn't have been there in person."

"It could be that he knew Bianchi," Erin said. "They might've been close. I haven't had a chance to look into their dealings."

"Make that your next step," Webb said. "There's a connection, I'd bet three packs of smokes on it. Moreno stuck his neck out for this."

"So did that dirty doc," Vic said. "Seems like they went into panic mode. Crazy, really. I mean, if all he had in his bloodstream was prescription meds, what the hell were they worried about?"

"Maybe they didn't know what killed him," Erin said. "And they assumed it was something that would cause trouble if we found it."

"Like what?" Webb asked.

"I don't know," Erin admitted.

"See if you can find out."

So Erin went back to her computer. While Vic kept going through bank records, she pulled Vincenzo Moreno's police jacket. It was thinner than it ought to be for such a senior figure in the Mob. He wasn't called the Oil Man for nothing. Vinnie had slipped out of the DA's clutches more than once. He'd done some time in his youth, eighteen months for assault. He'd been busted for a weapons charge once, twice for possession of heroin. None of it was unusual for a young gangster. Once he'd grown up, he'd either gotten more careful or gotten luckier. He'd kept his head down and his nose clean while quietly accumulating power and influence. He'd avoided the big cleanup of Mafiosi during the '90s, somehow dodging all the big RICO cases. When the dust had cleared, Vinnie the Oil Man was the tallest guy left standing amid the wreckage. Now the NYPD knew he ran the Lucarelli rackets in Manhattan; they just hadn't been able to prove it.

Once she had a sense of the guy, she checked Vinnie's file against Lorenzo's, looking for points of contact. She'd only just started looking when she got a hit.

"Hey, guys," she called. "Come over here."

"What's up?" Vic asked. "Let me guess. They killed Jimmy Hoffa, and you found out where he's buried."

"Not quite," Erin said. She wondered in passing whether Corky might have a story about what had happened to the infamous union leader. He'd just been a kid, still in Ireland, when Hoffa had vanished, but he did know lots of Teamsters bigwigs. General consensus was that the former Teamsters' president had been murdered by Irish hitman Frank Sheeran, but it had never been proven. She filed the thought away for future reference and brought her mind back to the current task.

"When Bianchi was running the Mafia's garbage business on Long Island, Vinnie worked for him," she said.

"Doing what?" Webb asked.

"On paper, he was a driver," Erin said, clicking through the pages of the file the NYPD had built on the garbage racket. "But it looks like he might've been into heroin distribution. The Narcs tried to build a case on Bianchi. They got some tips that his garbage business was a front for a drug network."

"What happened?"

"Insufficient evidence," Erin said. "Three of Bianchi's trucks got destroyed on their lot. Ammonium nitrate fuel oil explosives."

"Like the Oklahoma City bomb," Vic said.

"Or the IRA," Webb said, giving Erin a sharp look.

Erin didn't say anything. She was pretty sure her current boyfriend had built at least some of those bombs.

"So the Narcs gave up on it?" Vic asked.

"Yeah," she said. "Bianchi was out of the trash business after that. Anyway, he may have been some kind of mentor to Vinnie while the Oil Man was coming up through the ranks. And it sounds like both of them may have been in the drug trade."

"What, so he thinks Lorenzo died from shooting up heroin?" Vic demanded. "That's crazy. I've seen plenty of hop-heads, and Bianchi was clean. Cleaner than he should've been, you ask me. That guy could've used a little pick-me-up."

Erin was trying to think like a mobster. What would Carlyle say? He'd remind her the Mob was a business concern, first and foremost. People getting killed only mattered to them if it got in the way of business.

"What if there's something in the apartment?" she said suddenly.

"Huh?" Vic blinked at her.

"As long as we don't have enough evidence for a homicide investigation, we won't get a search warrant," Erin said. "That means we can't get our hands on whatever's in the apartment."

"What do you think is there?" Webb asked.

She shrugged. "Beats me. Drugs? Guns? A secret lasagna recipe?"

"Stop it," Vic said. "You're making me hungry."

"We've got to get eyes on that apartment," Erin said. "It might already be too late."

Webb nodded. "I'll call Patrol division, get them to send a plainclothes unit. Maybe we'll get lucky."

"I like plans that go, 'I hope we get lucky,'" Vic said. "Those are the best plans."

"Should we go over there?" Erin asked.

Webb shook his head. "I don't know that it matters," he said. "Maybe one of us can chaperone the Patrol guys."

"I'll do it," she said, before Vic could chime in. Anything was better than hanging around the office. Erin hadn't become a cop to ride a desk all day, and Rolf could use the exercise.

"Okay," Webb said. "I'll put you in touch with the plainclothes guys. Keep your eyes open, and will you please, as a personal favor, try not to get in any gunfights?"

"I'll give it my best shot," she said.

Vic grinned. "Word choice, O'Reilly. Word choice."

Chapter 11

Erin had plenty of time, over the course of that endless day, to reflect and regret that the only thing more boring than office work was manning a stakeout. She sat in her Charger, half a block down the street from the Bianchi apartment, and waited for something to happen. She couldn't read a book, or surf the Web on her phone, or catch up on paperwork. The whole job boiled down to keeping her eyes on the building and watching. She didn't even know precisely what she was looking for. Ultimately, it was anything that triggered her instincts, honed by more than a decade on the Patrol beat.

Another unmarked car was on the other side of the building, with a pair of officers doing the same thing she was. At least those two could have a conversation. Rolf was a great listener but didn't contribute much.

She glanced over her shoulder at the K-9. He was lying on the floor of his compartment, chin on his paws. He gave her a mournful look.

"Hey, it could be worse," she told him. "Most dogs have to sit at home all alone. At least you get to come with me."

The tip of his tail wagged slightly. He knew the words "come with." They were two of his favorites.

"I don't even know what the hell we're doing here," she said. "Unless they've got, like, two tons of cocaine in the basement, they probably shifted anything incriminating hours ago. Now we're just sitting here like assholes."

Rolf didn't disagree.

"I guess I could call someone while we wait," she said. "Ask some questions about drugs."

Rolf cocked his head at her.

"It's not just because he's my boyfriend," she said. "He might be able to help with this. And I don't need your permission." She pulled out her phone and called Carlyle. He changed burner phones every month or so, texting her the new number. She'd asked him about that, since the main reason for doing it was to avoid police attention and she was, in fact, a cop. He'd just shrugged and said it was force of habit. It was one of the quirks of dating a mobster.

"Afternoon," he said, picking up on the second ring.

"Hey there," she said. "Staying out of trouble?"

"If I'm not, you'll be the first to know."

"Are you somewhere you can talk?"

"I'm upstairs at the moment. If you must know, you caught me just out of the shower. I'd been to the gym, and now I'm sitting on my couch in a dressing gown, a glass of Scotch in my hand, talking to a sweet colleen. I daresay life could be a good deal worse. What is it you're wanting, darling?"

She smiled at the mental image. "They ought to use a picture of you in a cologne ad in Esquire," she said. "I'm afraid this is about work. I want to know about drugs."

"That's rather a broad topic, and one beyond the reach of my personal expertise."

"What do you know about Lorenzo Bianchi and Vinnie the Oil Man being involved in drug smuggling?"

"I heard some stories, back in the old days. My understanding is that Bianchi never had more than a sideline in the business. Strange to say, being a dustman was more lucrative."

"Dustman?"

"Garbage collector, darling."

"More money in garbage than drugs?"

"It's the world we live in," he said. "Not everyone takes drugs, but every household needs its waste hauled off. America's a culture of consumption, and that means it's a culture that throws a great many things away."

"So Lorenzo wouldn't have been in the drug-running business now, as far as you know?"

"Not that I've heard. I'll make inquiries. But from what I understand, it's his son that's a bit more in that line these days. Strictly small-time, of course."

Erin sat up in her car seat. "Paulie? Yeah, we thought he and Rocky Nicoletti might be into that. You hear much about them?"

"They're not big players," Carlyle said. "Go into a bad neighborhood and toss a half-brick. Odds are it'll land near a lad like him."

"So why would Vinnie be protecting him?"

"The Oil Man's a canny lad," he said. "He's a bit too young to be one of the true old guard of the Family, but he's one they look to as a man of respect. He has to keep them happy, while keeping abreast of the changing times. He's got one foot in each camp, old and new. It's a delicate balance he's keeping. I'd imagine he's wanting to curry favor with his boss by keeping Lorenzo's bairn out of trouble. Don't assume that means he actually cares what happens to the lad, however. Everything Vinnie Moreno does is for a particular tactical purpose."

"He's shoring up support with the old geezers," she said. "Gotcha. I think I better talk to our Narcotics guys. They may have something on the kid."

"Is this really your area, Erin? Chasing small-time drug dealers isn't precisely what the city's paying you to do."

"You're right," she said. "But what else am I supposed to do? I have to figure out the poisonings, and that means working out all the angles. We've got two dead so far, and I'm hoping we'll close this thing before any more bodies pile up."

"So Lorenzo was poisoned?"

"Looks that way."

"That's an unusual way for a lad in the game to throw in his cards."

"Murder is murder."

"True enough. You know, Erin, if you're not terribly busy, there's plenty of room on this couch beside me, and I've a bottle of Glen D that's nearly full."

"Thanks, but I'm still on duty."

"It's my job to tempt you into all manner of unwise behavior."

"And you're good at it," she chuckled. "I'll look you up at the end of my shift, okay? Save some of that bottle for me."

"Your name's on it. Best of luck, darling."

*   *   *

Then it was back to the waiting game. Some cops swore by coffee, gallons of the stuff, but Erin knew better. When you didn't want to leave the scene, even for a five-minute bathroom break, you wanted to go easy on the fluid intake. The boys in blue could use empty water bottles in an emergency, but the women had it tougher. Staying awake wasn't the main problem anyway. Distraction was the number one enemy. She couldn't let herself drift away with her thoughts. At least it was winter, so the car didn't overheat. It was gradually getting colder inside, but that wasn't as much of a problem, particularly for Rolf. If they'd been pulling this job in summer, she'd have had to keep the engine running for the air conditioning.

Why had she volunteered for this lousy assignment? Erin couldn't stand being in an office all day. She and Rolf had both needed to get out a little, even if it meant sitting curbside for a few hours. Sometimes it was just a lose-lose situation.

She keyed her radio and called the other car. "Hey, guys. O'Reilly here."

"Malinowski and Bauer," the reply came back. "Give us good news."

"You want good news?" she asked. "All is forgiven. Jesus died for our sins. Especially yours."

"Bauer's Jewish," Malinowski replied.

"So was Jesus."

He laughed. "What's up on your side of the street?"

"I got nothing. Just making sure you Patrol boys are still alive."

"Still breathing. Bauer needs a breath mint."

"So does Rolf."

"Want to trade partners?"

"Not on your life."

"Stay sharp, O'Reilly."

"You too, Malinowski."

The apartment door opened. Erin's head snapped up. Paulie Bianchi stepped outside. His hands were empty, but he was wearing a backpack over a light jacket.

The radio link was still open. "Guys!" she called. "I got the kid coming out."

"Copy that." Malinowski dropped his bantering tone. "You want us to roll to you?"

"Negative. You might spook him, and we still need eyes on the building. I got this." Erin didn't start the car. Paulie was on foot, walking quickly down the sidewalk. She didn't know where he was going, but driving slowly down the street behind him would be the most obvious thing she could do. On the other hand, he'd seen her before and would know her face. She'd stand out, especially if she took Rolf with her. She did a quick risk assessment and decided to tail him the old-fashioned way.

"Malinowski?"

"Go ahead."

"I'm leaving my vehicle and trailing Bianchi on foot, with my K-9."

"Copy that, O'Reilly. You need us, we'll be there. Be careful."

Erin waited until Bianchi was past her and looking the other way. Then she got out of the Charger and popped Rolf's compartment. The Shepherd hit the pavement ready for action, but he was disciplined. He stuck next to Erin's leg, not pulling on the leash. They started after the kid, hanging back about thirty feet, blending into the usual Manhattan pedestrian traffic.

Paulie wasn't a big kid, and Erin was only five foot six, so it was tricky keeping him in sight. But she didn't want to be spotted, so it was a tradeoff. She had to keep looking to the sides, making sure he didn't hop in a taxi or go into a storefront. It would've been easier if Rolf had his scent, but she didn't have any of Paulie's stuff for him to sniff.

She almost missed him, but she caught a sight of Paulie out of the corner of her eye as he went down into a subway entrance. "Great," she muttered. She'd been down on subways ever since she'd nearly been killed in a gunfight with Neo-Nazis in one the previous autumn. But she wasn't going to let bad memories stand in her way. She steered Rolf to the stairs. Paulie was moving fast and was already most of the way down. Erin sped up. Rolf trotted briskly beside her.

New York provided MetroCards to all its first responders, free of charge. Most cops didn't bother using them more than a few times a month, but there were definitely times it came in handy. Erin swiped her card a few seconds behind Paulie. They got onto the platform just as the train pulled in. Paulie hurried across the concrete and through the doors as soon as they opened. He turned as he climbed aboard. He and Erin made eye contact.

"Shit," Erin said, and saw Paulie's lips mouth the same word in almost perfect unison. Then she and Rolf were running across the platform. The doors were still open. Paulie was backing away. Then, as Erin and Rolf lunged onto the train, Paulie turned and sprinted down the length of the train car.

"Stop! NYPD!" Erin shouted. She hadn't been sure until that moment, but now she knew Paulie was up to something. The time for stealth was over.

Unfortunately, she also realized something else. Paulie was going to make it through the doors at the far end of the car and she wasn't. She was about to take a trip to the next station without him.

She made another quick decision. She wasn't fast enough, but maybe her partner was. Erin unsnapped his leash. "Rolf! *Fass!*"

The Shepherd uncoiled. He threaded between the legs of startled passengers as if it was an agility course. There were any number of people he could've bitten, but he'd been well trained and knew to go for the guy who was running. Even as the train's doors slid shut, he slipped through, his tail barely clearing the narrowing gap. As the train started moving, Erin saw a brief glimpse of the Mafia wannabe going down hard, Rolf on top of him.

Erin could have yanked the emergency stop. She wanted to. But she'd had it drummed into her by her dad that you did *not* do that unless the train itself was about to kill someone. It wasn't like the cord on a city bus that politely paged the driver to stop. It would automatically trigger extremely powerful compressed-air brakes. That would set a whole row of municipal dominoes falling, as the MTA would be contacted, the train wouldn't go anywhere for a quarter of an hour or more, and the brakes would need to be manually reset. At the very least, she'd have to fill out all kinds of forms and get her ass chewed by the MTA, the transit police, and Lieutenant Webb, in that order.

On the flip side, that meant she was stuck on the subway car, staring out the window at her K-9 who was locked in a clinch with a suspect. If Paulie had a gun, he might shoot Rolf.

"Damn, damn, damn," she said under her breath, her fingernails digging into her palms. She couldn't even call Dispatch on her phone. Rumor had it the city was working on installing wifi and cell service in the tunnels, but it hadn't happened yet. All she could do was wait and fret.

At the next station, she was the first one off the train. She saw a transit cop near the wall and ran toward him, holding up her shield.

"I need backup at the Canal Street Station!" she shouted. "Got a 10-12 by an unaccompanied K-9!"

A 10-12 meant a police officer was holding a suspect, which was more or less true. The cop gave her a surprised look, but called it in on his radio. By the time he got through, Erin was back in the tunnel, running alongside the track, sprinting back toward the previous station.

Breathing hard from her run, Erin vaulted onto the platform and saw a circle of bystanders keeping a cautious perimeter. A pair of uniforms had arrived a little before her, but they were clearly at a loss as to what to do. Neither one wanted to interfere with the dog, so they were contenting themselves with holding back the growing crowd. Paulie was still on the ground,

Rolf's jaws clamped on his arm. But the kid was smarter than Erin had given him credit for. Unlike many perps, he wasn't trying to pull free or fight back. He was holding perfectly still. As a result, while Rolf had him in a firm grip, the Shepherd wasn't cracking his bones. He'd have bruises, but that was about it.

"Okay, kiddo," Erin said. "You gonna hold still now?"

Paulie nodded cautiously.

"Rolf, *pust*," she said, giving him his "release" command. Rolf obediently let go of the kid and looked at Erin, wagging his tail and waiting to be told what a good boy he was. She pulled his special chew-toy out of her jacket pocket and tossed it to him. He dropped to his belly and started gnawing like an oversized puppy, to the delight of the onlookers. Several of them had their phones out and recording, and Erin knew her partner was on his way to becoming a social media celebrity.

Her attention was still on Paulie. "Show me your hands," she said. When he held out empty palms, she holstered her Glock. "Any weapons?"

"No."

"What's in the backpack?"

"Nothing. Just some stuff, is all."

"Right," she said. "I'm gonna need to take a look inside. Stay down and don't move, you understand?"

He nodded, giving Rolf a nervous glance. Both of them knew he didn't fancy another tangle with the K-9.

Erin had a legal right to search anybody in New York City, under the NYPD's stop-and-frisk policy. It was controversial, particularly when minorities were disproportionately targeted, but in these circumstances Erin figured she wasn't likely to get too much grief over it. It did mean more paperwork on her horizon. But that was a problem for later. For now, she wanted to see what was in the pack.

She was careful unzipping it. The last thing she needed was a needle-stick. She peeled back the outer flap.

"What the hell?" she murmured.

It was a box of convenience-store chocolates, identical to the one which had poisoned Norman Ridgeway.

"It's just candy, dammit," Paulie muttered. "Can I go now?"

Erin pulled out the box and turned it over in her hands. "How come it's not shrink-wrapped?" she asked.

"Huh?"

"Never mind." She opened the lid and found herself staring at about two dozen little plastic baggies, each of them containing white powder.

She looked down at Paulie. "It's candy, all right," she said. "You got the real sugar right here."

"I want a lawyer," he said. Under the circumstances, it was the smartest thing he could have said.

"Yeah, you do," she said. "Paulie Bianchi, you're under arrest for felony possession of narcotics. You need to hear your rights? I bet you know them, but I better give 'em to you anyway. Smile, you're on camera."

Three New Yorkers recorded Paulie's arrest on their phones, while seven more kept filming her dog. That was what passed for news these days.

Chapter 12

"My client has no comment at this time."

The Bianchi family's lawyer reminded Erin of a lizard in an expensive suit. His face was expressionless and she wasn't convinced he needed to blink. He was sitting beside Paulie in the interrogation room. Erin and Webb were on the other side of the table.

"Just so Mr. Bianchi understands how much trouble he's in," Webb said. "We've got him in possession of twenty-five bags of heroin. At an estimated fifty milligrams apiece, that's a gram and a quarter. That's short of an A-1 felony, but given your client's prior history of drug possession, he could be looking at fourteen years."

"I will be examining the chain of custody of the alleged narcotic," the lawyer said. "And I will be scrutinizing Detective O'Reilly's record to determine the likelihood that she planted the alleged narcotics on my client."

Erin bristled but knew better than to take the obvious bait.

"I will also be filing an excessive-force complaint against Detective O'Reilly," he went on. "Given the unsupervised attack of the dangerous animal which assaulted my client, I will be requesting it be destroyed."

"That's bullshit and you know it," Erin snapped. "Are you threatening an NYPD officer?"

Webb raised a calming hand. "Fortunately, the incident was captured on several civilian cameras, as well as security cameras in the subway," he said. "I'm sure the footage will dispel any such allegations."

"My office will bring a civil suit," the lawyer relentlessly continued, as if the detectives hadn't spoken. "I will also be filing complaints of police harassment. My client and his mother were accosted in a place of worship, immediately after the death of his father, and subjected to a humiliating interrogation."

"Your client is a suspect in an ongoing homicide investigation," Erin retorted. "And he's a drug dealer. I suppose the heroin was for emotional support in this difficult time?"

"My client has no comment," the lawyer repeated.

Webb stood up. "Thank you for your time," he said blandly. "We'll be charging your client shortly. You might want to stick around; it won't be long."

"But you can add the wait to your billable hours," Erin couldn't resist adding.

Once they were out of the interrogation room, and Bianchi's lawyer had gone downstairs to wait for them to finish charging the kid, Erin rounded on Webb.

"That asshole!" she exploded.

"Easy, O'Reilly," Webb said. "He's just doing his job."

"He threatened to kill Rolf! He's a damn Mafia goon, just like the jerks he works for!"

"Nothing's going to happen to Rolf," Webb said. "I saw the kid's arm. The teeth didn't even break the skin."

"And if he does try anything," Vic said, coming out of the observation room, "I'll help you beat the shit out of him."

"I'll pretend I didn't hear that," Webb said. "You know we can't beat up the lawyers."

"Hey, you wanna hear a joke?" Vic said. "What do you call a thousand lawyers at the bottom of the East River?"

Erin had heard this one. "A good start," she said. Then she followed up with one of her own. "I heard sharks don't eat lawyers. You know why?"

Vic snickered. "Professional courtesy. What's the difference between a defense attorney and a catfish? One's a scum-sucking bottom-feeder..."

"Okay, knock it off," Webb said. "And good work on the bust, O'Reilly."

"Yeah," Vic said. "You ever wash out of Major Crimes, you can go work for SNEU."

"Those guys are crazy," she said. "My dad always told me they were a bunch of nutjobs."

"Then you oughta fit right in," Vic said, grinning. "I always kinda wanted to be one of them."

"Unfortunately," Webb said, "this doesn't close our homicide."

"Yeah, Erin," Vic said, still grinning. "You gotta stop solving the wrong cases."

"But it has to be connected," she said. "I mean, the candy boxes were absolutely identical."

"I noticed that," Webb said. "But one of them had poisoned candy, the other had drugs. It'd have to be a hell of a coincidence for both boxes to be in the same apartment."

"But both boxes *were* in the same apartment," she reminded him.

"In that case, Rocky Nicoletti got the wrong box," Vic said.

Webb and Erin looked at him.

"I mean, Nicoletti's a small-time drug dealer," he said. "He'd have preferred the box of drugs, wouldn't he? So why did Paulie give him the other box?"

"Maybe he didn't mean to," Erin said. "Maybe Paulie gave him the wrong one, just like you said. By accident."

"What kind of idiot does a drug trade without looking in the box first?" Vic asked.

"The kind we've got in Interrogation Room One," Webb said dryly.

"So let's suppose Paulie's trying to get his drugs to Rocky," Erin said. "And he hides them in an empty candy box. Then he sees the box, assumes it's his, and gives it to his buddy. But the buddy opens it up later, and surprise! It's candy."

"So he gives the candy to his girlfriend," Vic said. "Not knowing it's poisoned."

"And she shares it with her other boyfriend," Erin said. "Not the classiest thing you could do. Next thing they know, he's dead."

Webb nodded. "Okay," he said. "But what happened to the other box in the meantime?"

"I expect Paulie had it hidden somewhere in the apartment," Erin said. "But he wouldn't have even thought to look for it before he knew it was still there."

"But why would he assume the other box was his?" Vic wondered. "If I was smuggling drugs and found somebody'd moved my shit around, I'd double-check."

"He's living with his mom," Erin said. "She probably cleans his room for him."

"What a loser," Vic said.

"But who put the other box in the apartment in the first place?" Webb asked.

"Nina," Erin said at once. "Vic and I think she killed Lorenzo."

"And the chocolate was her first try?" Webb asked.

"Yeah."

"Can you prove it?"

Erin and Vic glanced at one another.

Webb sighed. "That's a no."

"Not yet," Erin corrected him.

"And the drug bust is just a distraction from the homicide," he said.

"We could use it as leverage," Erin suggested.

"We could," Webb agreed, "if Paulie knew anything useful about the poison. But I don't think he does."

"I don't mean leverage on him," she said. As she said it, she felt dirty inside. There were times being a cop didn't feel all that different from being a gangster. "I mean Nina."

The other two detectives stared at Erin. "I've said it before, I'll say it again," Vic said in tones of respectful admiration. "You're one cold, hard bitch."

"Yeah," Webb said. "Mothers have a soft spot for their kids. Especially ones that are still living at home. It's a good idea, O'Reilly. You think Paulie's a momma's boy?"

"Probably," Vic said.

"So what do you think Mom's willing to do to keep her little boy out of prison?" Erin said, hating herself a little.

"Maybe tell the truth," Webb said. "I'll talk to the DA, see if we can get him to play ball."

* * *

As Erin climbed the stairs up to Major Crimes, her phone buzzed. She fished it out on the landing, letting the other detectives go on ahead.

"O'Reilly."

"Hello, darling."

"Hey," she said, glad she recognized Carlyle's accent. He didn't like to identify himself by name on the phone. "Miss me already?"

"Aye," he said. "But this is more of a business call."

She dropped her flirtatious tone. "What's up?"

"I know you were wanting a pleasant evening with me, but I've a fellow who's wanting a quiet word with you, when it's convenient. Perhaps at the end of the day?"

"This fellow have a name?"

"You saw him at a meeting on the subject of applied probability."

"Try that in English?"

"He's a card player, but not a particularly accomplished one. You'd recall a lad with a bit of a sniffle?"

"Oh, yeah. Him." She thought of Liam McIntyre, with his twitchy face and runny nose.

"Is there a problem, darling?"

"You'll understand if I'm a little less excited about seeing him than you."

Carlyle chuckled. "Aye, that's a fair point. What would you like me to tell him?"

She sighed. "Sure. I'll meet with him. But there better be a payoff."

"Darling, I'm shocked. I didn't think you wanted that sort of relationship."

"That wasn't what I meant!"

"I know what you meant." He sounded amused. "I'll make it up to you. Feel free to collect, at any time of your choosing."

"It's not like you to make an open-ended commitment like that."

"What can I say? You bring it out in me."

"Where does your guy want to meet?"

"Here at the Corner. Nine o' clock would be grand. Come around back."

"Okay, I'll be there."

"I'll have a drink poured and waiting."

* * *

"Good news," Webb said when Erin joined them in the office. "The DA would love to trade a low-level drug conviction for a murder collar. He's in. Shortest conversation I've ever had with him."

"Okay," Vic said. "Let's go get the bitch."

"Let's do this with a little tact, Neshenko," Webb said. "She's a grieving widow, remember."

"Who we think killed her husband," he shot back. "Don't they say crocodiles fake crying to put you off your guard?"

"I think that's an urban legend," Erin said.

"Urban crocodiles?" Vic said.

"Hey, it's New York," she said. "You've been down in the sewers. You know what it's like."

"Which is why I'm working Major Crimes and not Animal Control," he said. "So how about it, boss? We gonna get this girl, or what?"

"Okay," Webb said. "But just so we're clear, you are not playing good cop."

"That's okay," Vic said. "The bad cop gets to have all the fun."

* * *

They rolled up on the Bianchi apartment with just the three of them, plus Rolf. As Webb pointed out, one middle-aged woman shouldn't present too much of a threat to a full squad of NYPD detectives.

"I'm spending more time at this apartment than I am at home," Erin commented as the elevator whirred toward the top floor.

"Plenty of time to sit at home after we retire," Vic said. "Except the Lieutenant, here. He'll keel over from a coronary two weeks before he collects his pension. It'll be tragic, except for the irony of it."

"Half my heart trouble is because of you, Neshenko," Webb said. "If I kick off, I expect O'Reilly to put you away for manslaughter."

"Where's the other half come from?" Vic asked.

"It's a three-way split," Webb said. "Cigarettes, my second ex-wife, and O'Reilly."

"Why the second wife?" Erin asked.

Webb shook his head and sighed. "I did something stupid and married a lawyer the second time around. The first wife got the kids, the second one got the house."

"Ouch," Vic said. "So why don't you like lawyer jokes?"

"Lawyers hurt too much to be funny."

The elevator doors slid open. "We gonna take her downtown, or do it here?" Erin asked.

"We'll start here and see how it goes," Webb said. "I want her thinking about her kid, not about herself. We haul her into an interrogation room, she'll be thinking about her own chances."

"We've got no proof," she said quietly.

"She doesn't know that," he said and rang the doorbell.

A young Italian man answered the door. He was wearing a black suit and had slicked-back hair. From the look on his face, they weren't the people he was expecting.

"Who're you?" he asked sharply.

Webb held up his shield. "Lieutenant Webb, NYPD. We'd like to speak with Mrs. Bianchi."

"You got a warrant?"

"We're not searching the apartment, and she's not under arrest," Webb said. "A warrant isn't necessary."

"Take a hike," he said. "She ain't talkin' to you."

"And who, exactly, are you?" Webb asked.

"The guy who's tellin' you to get lost."

Vic cracked his knuckles and gave the other guy a long look. "What's your name?" he asked.

"I ain't tellin' you shit. And I don't have to."

"You know the rule book," Vic said. "You're right, you don't have to show us your ID. Of course, we can haul your ass down to the station and keep you there until we can ID you. But you probably know that already, since you're such a smart guy."

"Hey, Carlo!" Nina's strident voice called from the living room. "What's goin' on out there?"

"Carlo," Vic repeated. "See, that wasn't so hard."

Carlo scowled at them but didn't budge from the doorway. "She ain't takin' visitors." Then he called over his shoulder, "It's the police."

"That so?" she called back. A moment later, Nina Bianchi came into view like a black-clad, overweight force of nature. "Oh no you don't. You bastards. What, it wasn't enough to drive Lorenzo into a heart attack and arrest Paulie? Now you gotta come here again? You got a whole lotta nerve. I can't believe you got the guts to stand there on my doorstep and look me in the eye! You and your goddamn posse, with that bitch, her lousy fleabag, and that meathead. Get out of my house!"

"Ma'am," Webb said, without changing expression, "we're not inside your home. But if I could talk to you for a few minutes—"

"This is harassment," she went on. "I'm callin' my lawyer."

"I think that's a good idea, ma'am," Webb said. "He can advise you on your best option for avoiding prison time for your son."

"By the time he gets done with you," Nina said, "you'll be writing parking tickets in Albany. Whaddaya mean avoidin' prison?"

"You want to keep Paulie out of jail, don't you?" Webb asked quietly.

"Yeah? How you gonna help me do that?" Nina was obviously suspicious.

"Mrs. Bianchi," Carlo said. "I really think we oughta wait for Vinnie."

"Paulie has been charged with possession of heroin," Webb said. "We've got a deal for him, but it's good for a limited time. If we could just have a few minutes, it could save your son fourteen years of his life."

Nina's face blanched. "Fourteen years?" she echoed. Apparently no one had told her that piece of information.

Erin knew they'd won that round. The other woman sagged as some of the fight leaked out of her.

"Okay, come in," Nina said.

"I really don't think that's a good idea," Carlo said.

"Carlo, you ain't paid to think!" Nina retorted. "You're paid to do what you're told. You wanna talk to Vinnie? Go talk to Vinnie. This is my family we're talkin' about here. I'm gonna take care of my family. Get outta here, go run to the guy who does your thinkin' for you."

Carlo looked like he was going to protest, but he snapped his mouth shut. He shouldered past Webb and went toward the stairwell, pulling out a cell phone as he went.

"Thank you, ma'am," Webb said. "This shouldn't take long."

Erin hoped he was right. If that call was going where she thought, they were on a clock. The Oil Man or his henchmen would be showing up soon.

"And don't you try bein' all polite," Nina snapped. "I trust you more when you act like an asshole."

"Wow," Vic whispered in Erin's ear as they went inside. "It's like she knows him."

When they were assembled in the living room, Nina turned to face them, arms crossed. "Okay," she said. "I'm listenin.'"

"Mrs. Bianchi," Webb said. "I understand you're worried about your son, and I know this is a difficult time for you. We'd like to help Paulie, and we want you to help him."

"You wanna help my kid? After you get that mutt to chew on him and you haul his ass to jail? Bullshit."

"The important thing, ma'am, is that you want to help him," Erin said. "Paulie isn't the one we want."

"You don't want him? Then let him go."

"Mrs. Bianchi," Webb said. "We're not a Narcotics unit. We're Major Crimes. Our concern is to solve a murder."

"What murder? I dunno what you're talkin' about."

"It's two murders now, actually," Webb said. "The first one is a dentist, Norman Ridgeway."

"Never heard of him."

"He was poisoned," Erin said, watching Nina closely.

"That's tough for him," she said. "What's that got to do with me?"

"I thought we were talking about Paulie," Erin said quietly. "Not you."

She saw it then. Nina flinched just a little. *Gotcha*, Erin thought.

"I don't know nothin' about no dentist," Nina said, and the moment was gone.

Webb leaned forward. "What about Lorenzo Bianchi?"

"What about him?" Nina shot back.

"I suppose you don't know he was poisoned, too?"

"He died of a heart attack!"

"Caused by an overdose of his heart medication," Erin said.

"Lorenzo, God rest his soul, wasn't the most careful guy in the world," Nina snapped. "Maybe he took a couple extra pills."

"You had a family dinner the night he died," Erin said. "An unusual occasion, according to Paulie. You served spicy pasta sauce, which nicely covered the bitter taste of the pills."

"You're crazy!" Nina retorted. "You think I poisoned my whole family?"

"No, I don't," Erin said. "But I think you all got a dose of propranolol. And there's probably traces of it still in your system. How do you think that looks?"

"I don't care how it looks, 'cause you can't take my blood. You got no warrant."

"We don't need to take your blood," Erin said with a grim smile. "Because we've got Paulie."

"We have him on drug possession," Vic added, seeing where Erin was going with this. "We've got a warrant for him. If we find that drug in his system, and he was eating the same stuff his dad was..."

"You poisoned Lorenzo," Erin said. "Just tell us why. We've got a deal with the DA. Write out the statement, your kid walks on the drug charges."

"Free and clear," Webb added. "Not even probation. All charges will be dropped."

"You think I killed my husband?" Nina said.

"We know you did," Erin said. "What we don't know is why."

"I don't believe you," Nina said. "You ain't got nothin' on us that'll hold up in court. We got a good lawyer, he'll take you apart on the stand. I think we'll take our chances."

"We've got a witness who'll swear he got the poisoned candy from Paulie," Webb said softly. "That makes Paulie an accessory to murder, along with the drug charges. He's not looking at fourteen years. He's looking at the rest of his life behind bars."

Erin was waiting for Nina to crumble, for her defiance to collapse under the weight of all those years. But she'd misjudged the other woman. Nina didn't crumble; she exploded.

"You got any idea what it's like, livin' with a guy like Lorenzo? Yeah, you think it's great. He's got money, he's got respect, he's a big man, a man with a belly, you know? When we first hooked up, he's *somebody*, know what I mean? Guys take off their hats to him. Big guys, important guys, not just little nobodies. He's got the nice clothes, the fancy car. You think, this guy's goin' somewhere. And you climb in for the ride. The ride, it's okay, and hey, your looks ain't gonna last forever. I mean, sure, you're hot now, but just look at your mom, you'll see what you're gonna be one of these days.

"So you marry the chump, and next thing you know? You see he's just another asshole in a nice suit. You fight with him all the time, he slaps you around a little, you break some dishes, and then what? He retires!"

Nina rolled her eyes to give the ceiling a look of long suffering. "That's worse. I mean, before that, he's goin' places, he's out all night, sure he's ballin' the cocktail waitresses, but what guy ain't? Now he's home all the time, and you find out you can't stand each other. You fight until you get tired, then you just sit around and pretend you don't hate his guts and he don't hate yours. He's got no ambition, he's not goin' nowhere but down the drain. And you look in the mirror and see, this is your life! This lousy, no-good, has-been wiseguy is your husband. A bald, fat loser with a heart condition.

"But hey, it could be worse, right?" she went on, looking back at the detectives. "You got money, food on the table, a roof over your head. You can't get divorced, I mean, I'm a good Catholic, right? You get divorced, you go straight to hell!"

Vic gave Erin a quick look that asked what the rules were about divorce versus murder when it came to the afterlife. She smothered a smile.

"The worst thing is, the bastard's tryin' to kill me!" Nina finished.

All three detectives started. "Wait a second," Webb said. "Lorenzo was trying to kill you?"

"Of course he was!" Nina snapped. "What, you didn't see that look on his face when you were askin' him about the candy box? The candy he gave me for Valentine's Day? The hell kind of man tries to poison his wife on Valentine's Day? You see how quick he shut you down once you started askin' about that?"

"Lorenzo gave you the candy," Erin said.

"I just said that," Nina said. "When they give you a badge, do they forget to check your ears? Or your brains?"

"Why didn't you eat it?" Erin asked.

"I was gonna, but I had an appointment. I was gettin' a foot massage. So I set the box on the counter, and it was gone when I got back."

"What did you think had happened to it?" Webb asked.

"He wouldn't have eaten them himself. The man loved his wine and sausages, but he didn't care for chocolate. I thought maybe he gave them to his girlfriend."

"He had a girlfriend?" Webb asked.

Nina gave him a look that suggested he was the dumbest man she'd talked to in a very long time. She let the silence stretch out just long enough to make sure he got the message before going on.

"I didn't know Paulie took the box until you lousy coppers showed up here askin' all your damn questions. That's when I saw it in his face, and I knew what he was tryin' to do."

Erin silently cursed herself for missing Lorenzo's reaction. "How did you know Paulie wouldn't overdose on the heart meds like Lorenzo did?" she asked.

"You shittin' me? That boy don't respect his heritage." Nina tossed her head. "He don't go for home cooking. I knew he wouldn't take more than one helping. But Lorenzo never left food on his plate in his life."

"Just so we're perfectly clear," Webb said. "Paulie didn't know anything about any of this?"

"Not a thing," Nina said. "My boy's innocent."

"Except for the drug thing," Vic interjected.

Nina turned her tongue on Vic. "Shut up! You don't know nothin' about that! Your boss said they're droppin' the charges, so you don't say one word about my boy! Or I swear to Mary mother of God, I'll shove my foot so far up your ass it'll tickle your throat when I wiggle my toes!"

Vic raised his eyebrows. Nina braced her arms on her chair and looked like she was getting ready to carry out the threat.

"Everyone take it easy," Webb said, holding up his hands. "We've got what we need here. Mrs. Bianchi, we're going to need you to come down to the station and fill out a statement confirming what you've just told us. The district attorney will be there, and he can verify the deal."

"Can I see my boy?"

"Once we've got the statement, he'll be released," he assured her. "You can have a few minutes with him then. I promise."

Vic stood up and took out his handcuffs. "Ma'am, I'm going to need you to turn around," he said.

"You need those, big guy?" she asked contemptuously. "What, you think you couldn't take me without 'em?"

"It's protocol," he said.

"Mrs. Bianchi," Erin said. "You're under arrest for first-degree murder. You have the right to remain silent..."

As she finished the familiar recitation, Vic snapped the bracelets on the Italian woman. Nina didn't resist. She didn't even seem angry anymore. As they walked her to the door, Erin on one side, Vic on the other, Rolf flanking his partner, Erin saw a smile on Nina's face.

"Something funny?" she asked.

"I been married to a Mafia goon for going on thirty years," Nina said. "And I finally made my bones. Take a good look, boys. Nina Bianchi just got made!" Then she actually laughed.

Webb went ahead to call the elevator. He'd scarcely pushed the button when the doors slid open to reveal three men: the Bianchi family lawyer, Carlo, and Vinnie the Oil Man.

"Well, this is awkward," Vic muttered. He took a step to the side, freeing up his gun hand. Erin kept a grip on Nina's arm with one hand and dropped her other to her holstered Glock. Rolf, sensing the mood, raised his hackles and tensed.

"This is a surprise," Vinnie said softly. "I have to say, Lieutenant, I wasn't expecting you to target a widow this way."

"She's under arrest," Webb said. "If you'd care to step aside?"

Vinnie didn't move. His voice was as smooth and cultured as ever, but there was a cold, hard edge to it now. "I don't claim to understand how things work in your sphere, Lieutenant Webb, but in mine, family members are off-limits."

"Sorry, Mr. Moreno," Webb said. "That's not in our Patrol Guide."

"You do the crime, you do the time," Vic added.

"I'll be sure to remember all of this," Vinnie said. "I do hope you haven't told them anything which could cause problems, Mrs. Bianchi."

Nina gave him a scornful look. "I got made, you slick son of a bitch," she said. "But don't worry, I'm stand-up. I did what I did, and I'm doin' the time. Put that in your pipe and smoke it."

"Mrs. Bianchi," the lawyer said, "don't say another word. Not one."

Webb turned to the attorney. "We're going to Precinct 8," he said. "If you'd care to follow us, I'm sure you'll find plenty to keep you busy."

"Lots and lots of billable hours," Vic said, giving Erin a sly smile.

Chapter 13

Getting Nina booked and sorting out the deal with the DA for Paulie's release took the rest of the day and part of the evening. The Bianchi lawyer tried his best, but Nina wasn't interested in his attempts to obstruct the process. She was proud of what she'd done, she said, and she'd do it again.

Up in Major Crimes, Vic and Erin started boxing up the evidence, getting ready for the next case. Webb, as the ranking officer from the arrest, was filling out the lion's share of the paperwork. Vic looked downright cheerful for a change.

"You're happy," Erin said. "Considering you didn't get to beat anyone up or shoot anybody."

He paused. "Erin, you really think I like shooting people?"

"I can see how a guy might think you did," she said.

"Jesus." He set down the file box he'd been holding. "You seriously think I get up in the morning and think, 'Gee! I hope I get to shoot someone today!' The hell is the matter with you? I'm not a goddamn psycho. I like the action, I like the juice, sure. I don't mind mixing it up, throwing a perp across the room, but gunning down mopes is not how I get my kicks."

Erin was taken aback. "I didn't mean..." she began.

"I know, I know. I'm just Vic the crazy Russian, the guy who was too nuts for ESU. You have any idea how many guys I could shoot, without breaking the rules? Shit, when I was working ESU, I'd throw down on guys six, seven times a week. That's every day, practically. Know how many times I fired my gun in the line, before I came to work with you?"

"Zero?" Erin guessed.

"Zero," he confirmed. "So maybe I'm not as psycho as all that. Maybe we've just got a curse on us here in Major Crimes. Since I took up with you crazy bastards, I get in gunfights all the damn time. I've been shot more than once. I've taken guys down hard. And today I'm in a good mood because I *didn't* have to mow down a perp. Or at least I was. So get off my back, okay?"

Erin held up her hands. "Okay, I get it," she said. "Sorry. It was a good collar and a good case."

"One thing I'm wondering, though," Vic said.

"By all means, elaborate," Webb called from behind his desk. "Every clean, tidy case needs some loose ends tied onto it. We're only two hours past quitting time as it is."

"Why was that slick Italian bastard so keen to shut this thing down?" Vic asked, ignoring his boss's sarcasm.

Erin had been thinking about that, too. "I have a theory," she said.

"Enlighten us," Webb said.

"I think he knew Nina killed Lorenzo," she said. "Or at least he suspected it."

"How the hell would he know?" Vic demanded.

She shrugged. "Doesn't matter. Just suppose for a minute he did. What was a guy like him gonna do in that situation? He'd protect his organization. If we figured out Nina was the killer, what would stop her making a deal with us?"

"She did make a deal with us," Vic said, giving Erin a funny look. "You were in the room. Were you paying attention?"

"That's not what she means," Webb said. "O'Reilly's talking about Nina giving up dirt on the Lucarelli family."

Vic blinked. "Oh." For once, he didn't have a smart remark.

"Sure, she's not directly connected," Erin said. "But she was married to a wiseguy for three decades. How much dirty laundry you think got aired around her in all that time?"

"You think she knows where the bodies are buried?" Webb asked.

"Some of them," she said.

"Shit," Vic said. "That's a great idea. We gotta flip that girl."

"We'll try," Webb said. "She's already admitted to the crime. Now it's up to the DA to work out a separate plea deal with her. I'll have a talk with him. Maybe he can get her to play ball, for her own sake."

"That's what I think Vinnie's worried about," Erin agreed. "He wanted to keep her out of jail so she wouldn't have a reason to talk to us."

"You heard what she told him," Vic said. "She said she was stand-up, that she wouldn't squeal on anyone."

"Lots of perps say that at first," Webb said. "Then they start staring down the length of all those years."

"I guess maybe we're not done with her yet," Vic said. "You want us to leave this stuff out?"

"Don't file it away just yet," Webb said. "Let's see what develops. But we're done for tonight. Good work, people."

"Buy me a drink?" Vic asked Erin as they headed for the stairs.

"Why would I do that?"

"To apologize for being a bitch."

She grinned at him. "To you? Never."

"Okay, I'll get the second round," he said.

"Not tonight," she said, remembering. "I've got a thing I need to do."

"Getting laid?"

"No!"

"You're totally getting laid."

"You'd say that whatever I said."

He shrugged. "Probably."

"It's nothing like that," she said. "I'm meeting an informant."

"Oh." Vic was suddenly serious. "You want some backup?"

"That's okay," she said. "I got this."

"You sure?"

"Hey. It's me."

"Yeah, it's you," he said. "Sometimes when you go to meet informants you find bombs, or Nazi gunmen."

"No Nazis tonight."

"Promise?"

"You worried about me?"

"I'm worried I'll miss out on the fun."

"Okay, Vic. I promise, the next time I'm going to get in a fight with neo-Nazis, I'll call you first."

"Deal. Take care of yourself, O'Reilly."

"Back at you."

*   *   *

Erin was feeling good when she walked down the alley to the Corner's back door. Two homicides were cleared, one perp deceased, the other in custody. That was a fine day's work by any detective's standards. She had Rolf at her side, and she'd be seeing her boyfriend soon. Granted, they had to clear up whatever business Liam had, but she was looking forward to a pleasant evening after.

Ian wasn't on duty. Caleb, another of Carlyle's security guys, let her in. He was a typical Irish Mob guy; heavyset, tough-looking, tattooed.

"Where's your boss?" she asked.

"Back room," he grunted.

Erin nodded, went to the indicated door, and knocked.

The door swung open and Erin's good feeling vanished. She was staring up into Mickey Connor's flat, cold eyes. The O'Malley enforcer filled the doorway. He looked down at her. She looked back. Neither one spoke for a moment.

"You gonna stand there all night?" Erin finally asked.

Mickey made a sound that might have been either a snort or a low laugh, but there was no hint of a smile. "What're you doing here?" he asked.

"What're *you* doing here?" she shot back. "I was invited." But her thoughts were racing. Had something happened to Carlyle? Was she about to get jumped? She wondered how fast Mickey was. Could she clear her Glock before he got his hands on her? How many shots would it take to put that big body down?

"Mickey," Carlyle's voice came from behind Mickey. "She's the reason we're here tonight. I'm thinking you should let her in."

"I don't work for you," Mickey said over his shoulder, without taking his eyes off Erin.

"It was a suggestion, not an order," Carlyle said quietly. "But if it's orders you're wanting, I'm certain we can get Evan on the telephone."

Mickey's eyes finally shifted. A moment later, so did his body, making a path for Erin. She had to pass closer to him than she wanted. She caught a faint scent of sweat and cheap deodorant. Standing within a few inches of him, she could feel the physical menace that radiated off the man. Every instinct in her screamed to get away from him. She pretended not to feel the perfectly rational fear, keeping her face impassive. She even let herself give him a ghost of a smile. She remembered her dad's advice for dealing with street thugs.

"They're like a pack of stray dogs. If they smell fear on you, you're done. You gotta make them think you're braver than they are. Or, if you can't manage that, make them think you're crazier than them. They respect crazy people."

Rolf didn't feel the need to be as subtle as Erin. His hackles rose when he looked at Mickey and a low rumble came from his chest.

Carlyle was sitting at the card table, opposite Liam McIntyre. On the table was a pair of glasses and a bottle of Glen D whiskey. Liam had a soda glass in front of him, filled with the same godawful chocolate liquor concoction he'd had poker night, a "death by chocolate." It was topped with whipped cream and a maraschino cherry.

Carlyle stood up to greet her. Liam didn't. Mickey leaned against the wall by the door and crossed his arms over his chest.

"So," Erin said, still pretending to be nonchalant. "What're we doing here?" She slid into the seat on Carlyle's left. He was already pouring her a drink. She took a sip, only a small one. This was one time she really wanted a clear head.

"Liam has something to say to you, Erin," Carlyle said.

"I'm here," she said. "Start talking."

Liam gave her a quick glance. He seemed unable to hold steady eye contact. He was one of the twitchiest guys she'd seen, with the same manner as a hardcore meth tweaker.

"We cool?" he muttered. "I mean, Cars says you're cool, but I gotta know, right? 'Cause if we're doin' business, we gotta have, like, an understanding."

"Liam," Erin said, leaning forward. "Relax, okay? What is it you need?"

"I heard there's somethin' goin' down," he said, shooting her another furtive, bloodshot look. "There's some shit gettin' moved."

"When?"

"Tonight."

"How much weight?"

"Ten, twelve kees of H. Colombian, good shit. Ninety-five percent pure."

Erin did some quick math in her head. Twelve kilograms of high-quality South American heroin could wholesale for a million dollars, give or take. Not the biggest haul in law-enforcement history, not by a long shot, but significant.

"Who's moving the product?" she asked.

Liam shifted uncomfortably. He really wasn't used to talking business with cops.

"Lad," Carlyle said quietly, "it's all right. This is precisely the sort of thing Erin can help with."

"Italian guys," Liam said in a quick, low voice. "Lucarellis."

"Where's this going down?" Erin asked.

"East River docks."

"You got the dock number?"

"Pretty close."

"Liam," Erin said, "pretty close isn't good enough."

"It don't matter," Liam said. "I know how they're movin' the shit downtown."

"How?"

"It'll be in a delivery truck. Marked Speedy X-Press. That's an 'X' and then 'Press.'"

"You know where they're going?"

"Little Italy. They'll probably take Saint James to Bowery to Canal."

Erin looked closely at the nervous little guy. "You know a lot about this move. How good is your info?"

Liam's eyes flicked toward Mickey, then Carlyle, then down to his own hands. "I talked to a guy."

"How many guys in the truck?"

He shrugged. "Dunno. Two, probably."

"Armed?"

He shrugged again. "Probably."

"What time is the pickup?"

"Dunno. Depends. Could be in half an hour, could be an hour, maybe two."

Erin stood up. "Okay. Thanks. I'll call it in."

Mickey took a step away from the wall. "Who you gonna call?" he growled.

"My people," she said.

"And tell 'em what?" he retorted. "The Oil Man finds out Liam told you this, you're gonna be pullin' him outta the East River in a day or two."

"Then what the hell did you call me here for?" Erin shot back.

"I didn't want to call you. Cars said you take care of things for him. Take care of this."

"That's what I'm doing."

"Not your people." Mickey uncrossed his arms and thrust one massive finger at her. "You."

"That's not how the NYPD does things," she said. "I'm not going to take down a couple of armed thugs by myself on your say-so."

Mickey nodded. "That's what I told him," he said. "Take away the badge and you're just a naked pu—"

"Careful, Mick," Carlyle interrupted in a deceptively soft tone. "You open that door, I don't think you'll like what's behind it."

Erin sized up the man in front of her. She could ignore Mickey's instructions. Chances were, he'd let her and Rolf walk out without a fight. By herself, she didn't think she could take him, but with her K-9 she bet she could. But that wasn't the point. This was a test, to show Evan O'Malley how useful she could be. If she fought with Mickey, the O'Malleys wouldn't trust her, and that could get both her and Carlyle killed down the road.

"Okay," she said. "I'll keep Liam's name out of this. I can play it as a tip from a guy we snagged earlier. I won't say a word about this meeting. But I have to bring the Narcs in. I'm going to need a few more bodies to make the stop. And I have to get on this now, if you want me to get it done. So, would you mind getting out of my way?"

Mickey didn't smile, but he did nod to her with just a little respect. And he stepped aside.

"Catch you later," she said to Carlyle.

"Thank you, Erin," he said, rising. "Be careful."

*   *   *

If Erin had really wanted to be careful, she wouldn't have found herself meeting up with the Street Narcotics Enforcement Unit. SNEU had a reputation for reckless behavior, as Erin's dad had warned her. But they were also unconventional enough to go along with a tip from a dodgy source in Major Crimes on very short notice. Erin knew Lieutenant Webb would be pissed at being kept out of the loop, but there wasn't time to explain up the chain of command. She got in touch with Narcotics, who patched her through to Sergeant Logan, one of the guys on duty on the Lower East Side. She called him from her car, already en route.

"Logan here." He sounded awake and alert. It was middle evening, about nine thirty. For a street Narc, the workday was just getting going.

"This is O'Reilly, Major Crimes," she said. "I got a hot tip. You got some guys willing to make a street bust?"

"Hell yeah. How much weight?"

"Could be twelve kilos."

"I'm in," Logan said. "Where and when?"

"It'll be in a truck on Saint James, headed toward Bowery. It's happening soon, sometime in the next couple hours."

"Copy that. I can have my guys there in twenty. Meet you at Triangle Park, next to the cemetery?"

"Copy," Erin said. "These guys may be armed, so be ready to come heavy."

"Copy, O'Reilly. See you there."

Chapter 14

Sergeant Logan and his squad were hanging around the Saint James Triangle Park when Erin got there, looking like overage delinquents.

"Okay," Erin said. "Which one of you cowboys is Logan?"

"O'Reilly?" Logan said, coming forward and offering his hand. He was a tall, lanky guy with a black leather jacket and a silver skull earring. "Glad to meet you. Paul Logan. This is Janovich, Firelli, and Piekarski."

The three other Narcotics officers, two men and a woman, nodded greetings. Erin could tell they were wearing bulletproof vests under their coats. She'd put on her own body armor in the car. Rolf had his vest, too, which spoiled the plainclothes effect for him.

"You better get that K-9 out of sight," Logan said. "How you wanna play this?"

"It'll be two wiseguys in the truck," she said. "Maybe do a surprise roadblock?"

"Yeah," he said. "I figure we'll put Piekarski up the block. She'll call it in when she makes the vehicle. Then Firelli pulls out of that space there and blocks the street. Then you,

Janovich, me, and the dog take 'em from both sides. Quick and hard, don't give 'em a chance to resist."

"Sounds good," Erin said. "The truck's going to be labeled 'Speedy X-Press.' You got that, Piekarski?"

Piekarski, a petite blonde in an old denim coat, grinned and winked. "Gotcha covered. I'll give you a block's worth of lead time."

"Everyone make sure you got your radios up," Logan said. "O'Reilly, you want to wait in your car with your dog?"

"Sure," she said. "You and Janovich going across the street?"

"Yeah," Logan said. "Okay, let's set 'em up and knock 'em down, people."

Logan and Janovich put their hands in their pockets and strolled across the street, acting like just a couple of ordinary New Yorkers. They leaned casually against the wall of the building across from the park and settled into a conversation.

Firelli glanced at Erin. "You ready to roll with us, O'Reilly?"

"Absolutely."

"Shit's gonna move fast once it gets rolling," he said. "This ain't paperwork, desk jockey."

"I'm a detective," she reminded him. "I work for a living."

He smiled, showing a gap where one of his front teeth should've been. "Whatever you say. Just jump when we jump." He walked to his car, a beat-up old Trans Am, spray-painted black. He got in and closed the door, leaving the engine off.

Erin put Rolf back in his compartment in her Charger and settled into the driver's seat. Then it was time to wait again. At least this stakeout had an endpoint. If the truck didn't show, or had already passed before they'd gotten there, they wouldn't have to stay all night. She'd give it until midnight, she decided. If the truck didn't show by then, it wasn't going to.

"Desk jockey," she muttered to Rolf. "You believe that?"

He put his snout between his front paws and stared at her.

"Com check," Logan's voice came over the radio.

"Firelli here."

"Piekarski."

"Janovich."

Erin punched her car radio. "O'Reilly."

"Okay," Logan said. "Remember, this goes on Wopstat for the month."

"Eat me, Irish," Firelli said.

"What's Wopstat?" Erin asked.

"Logan and Firelli got a pool running," Janovich explained. "They keep count how many Irish and Italian guys they bust. Firelli counts the Irish, calls 'em Mickstat. Logan counts the Italians..."

"Got it," Erin said.

"It's just the ethnic groups we got on the squad," Logan said. "If we busted enough Polacks, we'd have a Polestat for Piekarski, but for some reason we don't get many of them."

"That's 'cause we're too smart to get caught," Piekarski said.

"That reminds me of a joke," Janovich said. "So, this Polish guy's in a bar, watching the evening news, and they're talking about this guy who's gonna jump off the Empire State Building—"

"Enough of that," Logan said. "Save the jokes for later, and keep the channel clear. Just remember, if these guys are Italians, Firelli's buying first round."

Firelli muttered something uncomplimentary under his breath and silence returned to the radio net.

Erin sat back and smiled, thinking how much she sometimes missed ordinary street police work, the rough camaraderie, the sorts of things you could only say to guys you risked your life to protect, and who'd risk theirs to save you. She had that with Vic, but he was about the only one at Precinct 8. She'd been more and more isolated, and now, having lost Kira

Jones to Internal Affairs, there just weren't many people she
could talk to at work.

Time crawled. Erin thought about Liam, and Mickey, and
Carlyle. Whatever happened tonight, her relationship with the
O'Malleys was changing. If the NYPD got a good bust out of it,
that wouldn't do her any harm, but what about the next thing
they asked her to do? The whole business felt like it was right
on the ragged edge of control. One slip and the whole thing
might spin out from under her. She'd have to sort this shit out,
and soon.

"Heads up, guys," Piekarski said. "I got a truck... no, forget
about it. Says 'Speedy Delivery.' You sure about the name,
O'Reilly?"

"I know what they told me," she said.

They returned to their wait. Half an hour passed, then an
hour. There was no sign of the promised vehicle.

*   *   *

"Wake up, fellas!"

Erin jerked upright. Piekarski sounded excited.

"I got a white truck," the Narc continued. "Red letters,
'Speedy X-Press' on the side, coming your way."

"Copy that," Logan said. "Everyone ready?"

"Ready," Erin said, her voice overlapping with Firelli and
Janovich.

"Okay," Logan said. "Firelli, you got the lead. Everyone else,
move when the truck stops. Guns out. Violence of execution,
people."

Erin knew Logan wasn't actually talking about violent
executions. He meant they needed to move fast and hard, to
overwhelm the targets with a show of force so they wouldn't
even have a chance to consider resistance. Paradoxically, if done

right, it would mean very little, if any, actual violence. She drew her Glock and put a hand on the car door, feeling the familiar tingle of adrenaline.

The delivery truck was halfway up the block, moving with the flow of traffic. Taxis and other cars filled the street. Erin saw an awful lot of innocent bystanders. She hoped shots wouldn't be fired. It was far too easy to imagine a stray round taking out some poor guy on his way home. She licked her lips and waited. She saw Firelli's Trans Am start up, idling curbside.

Firelli let all but one of the cars in front of the truck go by. Then he abruptly threw the Trans Am into gear and swerved halfway out of his parking space, angling the car directly across the traffic lane. The car he'd cut off screeched to a halt, brakes screaming. The driver, predictably, laid down a heavy blast on his horn. Every other car behind, including the delivery truck, jolted to a halt, instantly gridlocked.

"Go!" Logan snapped.

Erin was already moving. She came out of the Charger, keying Rolf's compartment release as she went. The truck was only a few feet away. She sprinted to the passenger side, reached up to grab the rearview mirror, and pulled herself up to window height. She shoved the barrel of her Glock against the glass and saw a very startled face staring back at her from the passenger seat.

"NYPD!" she shouted. "Hands in the air! Now!" On the other side of the truck, Janovich was doing pretty much the same thing to the driver. Logan stepped toward the front bumper so he could cover both guys through the windshield.

The guy facing Erin blinked a couple of times and considered his options, but only for a second. Then he brought up his hands, empty and open, and laid his palms on the dashboard. The driver was already holding the steering wheel, looking straight ahead.

"Unlock the doors!" Janovich shouted.

Maybe the driver would've done it, but Janovich didn't give him time. Still holding his gun on the driver with one hand, he slammed his other hand into the window. The glass shattered into tiny pebbles that sparkled under the streetlights. Erin saw a safety hammer glass-breaker in Janovich's hand and wished she'd thought of that. The Narc punched through the broken window and unlocked the driver's side door. He pulled it open and hit the unlock button for Erin's side.

"Get out of the car!" he shouted at the two guys. "Keep your hands in the air!"

The men seemed dazed by what had happened. They offered no resistance whatsoever as Erin, Janovich, and Logan laid them against the hood of their truck and frisked them. Firelli and Piekarski had arrived by then, Piekarski having sprinted down the sidewalk. The two of them, plus Rolf, established a perimeter to keep the rubberneckers at a safe distance.

"What've we got here?" Logan said, pulling a revolver out of the driver's waistband.

"That's for protection," the driver said.

Erin's frisk of her guy turned up a nine-millimeter Beretta. "Got another gun here, Sarge," she said to Logan.

"That's a whole lotta protection," Logan said. "What're you protecting?"

"Nothin'," the driver said. "Just normal delivery."

"Then you won't mind if we take a look," Logan said.

"You got a warrant?"

"Don't need a warrant. We got you on a weapons charge already. Gives us plenty of cause to search the vehicle. Janovich, cuff this guy."

Erin snapped her bracelets on her man. "What's your name?" she asked him.

He didn't say anything. Now that he'd recovered a little from his surprise, he just glared at her. He was a youngish man, probably in his early twenties, and definitely looked Italian. She glanced at Firelli.

"Afraid you're buying," she said to him.

Firelli shrugged. "That's okay. Logan got the last one."

To the accompaniment of increasingly irritated honking of car horns, they finished securing the prisoners and opened the truck's loading door.

Someone primed by Hollywood images of drug busts would've been expecting the whole back of the truck to be full of bags stuffed with white powder. But Erin knew twelve kilograms didn't take up that much space. What she saw, when the door rolled up into the ceiling of the truck, was boxes of chocolate.

"Candy?" Logan said, looking over Erin's shoulder.

"Candy," she agreed. She pulled on a pair of latex gloves and climbed into the truck. She opened the first box she came to, holding it toward Logan. "Hungry?"

He looked at the small baggies of powder inside and grinned. "Starving."

Chapter 15

"So," Logan said. "Who gets the collar? SNEU or Major Crimes?"

"You can have it," Erin said.

They'd moved the truck to the side of Saint James so traffic could get moving again. Now they were standing in the park, looking at about a million dollars' worth of heroin spread on a wooden bench.

"You sure?" Piekarski asked. "This is a solid bust, good weight, plus the guns. It's gonna look good on your record."

Erin shrugged. "It kinda fell into my lap," she said. "Besides, it may be better if this is a Narcotics op."

"Protecting a source?" Logan asked, giving her a keen look.

"Something like that."

"I'm not gonna lie," he said. "You want to give us this, we'll take it. Hell, I'll take a double felony collar with this kind of weight any night of the week. But I gotta have something to put on my DD-5s for the reason for the stop."

"Okay," she said, recognizing it wouldn't be possible to keep Major Crimes entirely out of the paperwork. "We've been working a narcotics angle on a dual homicide, connected to the Lucarellis. Say we got a tipoff from one of the Lucarelli sources."

"Sounds good to me," Logan said. "It's obvious you had good intel. I'm a little surprised you didn't work through Precinct 8."

"We're in Precinct 5 territory," she said. "It'd be rude for the Eightball's Narcs to roll on your turf."

Logan nodded, but looked unconvinced. He knew she wasn't giving him the whole story.

"Hey, Sarge," Firelli said. "O'Reilly's giving us this righteous collar, I think she gets an invite to the bar at the end of the shift."

"What time's your shift end?" Erin asked.

"Depends," Janovich said. "You ever work the dog watch?"

"All the time," she said, scratching Rolf behind the ears.

"Then you know how it goes. Rack up an hour or two of unpaid overtime."

"Tell you what," Firelli said. "If you're up early..."

"Or still awake..." Piekarski added.

"...we'll be at the Final Countdown at six," Firelli finished.

"That's 0600," Janovich clarified.

"For drinks," Erin said, deadpan.

"Damn right," Firelli said. "Not beer, either. We're talking straight shots."

"Maybe," she said. "You guys will be ending your shift. I'll be starting mine. But what about the liquor laws?"

Piekarski laughed. "It's more of a club than a bar, that time of morning," she said. "The barkeep's a retired cop, runs a special service for officers who work nights. It's not open to the public."

"Isn't that still illegal?" Erin asked.

The SNEU team looked at each other and shrugged.

"If you change your mind, you know where to find us," Logan said. "And Firelli's buying the first round, remember." He offered his hand. "Y'know, it occurs to me, you could just be throwing us this collar to dodge the paperwork."

"Is it working?" she asked, smiling at him and shaking hands.

"This time," he said, returning the smile. "Take it easy, O'Reilly."

*   *   *

With the prisoners handed over to SNEU and the drugs on the way to Precinct 5's evidence locker, it was back to the Barley Corner for Erin. She wasn't sure what to expect. Being honest with herself, she was a little pissed at Carlyle for blindsiding her.

She went in the front door this time. What was the point in sneaking around back? The O'Malleys already knew about her, and Vinnie's Mafia goons would hardly be hanging out at the Corner. She and Rolf walked right in like they owned the place.

They almost ran into Corky on his way out. With that smooth, astonishing speed he had, the Irishman nimbly sidestepped and touched a finger to his forehead in salute.

"Evening, love," he said. "If you're looking for the publican, you'll find him upstairs." He lowered his voice a little. "He's not given you a key, has he?"

Erin smiled thinly. "No, Corky, he hasn't."

"I think he's expecting you," Corky said. "I'd stay for a chinwag, but we've both business to attend to. I'll be seeing you, love."

She crossed the main room, trying to identify the wiseguys. She recognized a couple of O'Malley goons at the bar, and a side booth had four more. She hoped they were all Carlyle's guys, not Mickey's. At least Mickey Connor wasn't present.

The door to Carlyle's upstairs apartment was a solid piece of engineering. Since she didn't have a spare key, as she'd told Corky, she needed either a cutting torch, a big chunk of explosives, or for him to open the door for her. She pushed the bell on the intercom.

"Evening," his voice came from the speaker.

"It's me," she said. "I'm back."

"Grand," he said. "Come on up." The door's heavy bolts clanked back. She opened the door and climbed the stairs, Rolf keeping pace.

Carlyle was looking disheveled. By his standards, this meant he'd taken off his suit coat and slightly loosened his tie. He was in the living room, a glass of whiskey in each hand. He extended one to her. She took it and knocked back a mouthful, savoring the fierce heat in her throat.

"You look well," he said. "No trouble, I take it?"

"It went down fine," she said. "Just the way Liam said it would. Look, Carlyle, what are we doing here?"

"Sharing a nightcap," he said, motioning her to the couch.

She took a seat, but kept her back straight, sitting on the edge of the cushion. Rolf eyed her warily, sensing her nervous energy. Carlyle surely saw it too, but he gave no outward sign. He sat beside her on the couch and took a sip of his own drink.

"What the hell was Mickey doing here?" she burst out.

"Observing," Carlyle said.

"Who? Me? You?"

"Both, I imagine."

"Whose idea was this?"

"To what, precisely, are you referring?"

"Can we put away the bullshit, just for tonight?" she asked.

He smiled. "Old habits, darling. But I assume you're talking about the tipoff regarding a shipment of illegal narcotics?"

"Yeah."

"I'm not certain. Liam came to me with his information, but I'm thinking it wasn't his brainchild. You may have noticed, he's not precisely the most well-balanced lad in the family."

"He'll be dead or in prison in two years," Erin predicted. "Maybe less."

"Probably," Carlyle agreed. "Given Mickey's presence, I've an idea Liam was operating on Evan's instructions. So you know, I'd no idea he'd be coming until he showed up on my doorstep. I'd have warned you otherwise. He's rather an alarming lad to come upon unexpectedly."

"He is that," Erin said. "So what was it, another test?"

"Partially," Carlyle said. "I think Evan's feeling you out, finding what you can and can't be relied upon to do for him."

"I don't work for him," she said, bristling. "Hell, I don't work for you."

"I know that, Erin," he said, laying a hand on her wrist.

His touch was gentle, but she still almost threw him off. "Do you?"

"Aye," he said. "It's simply part of the difficult situation in which we find ourselves. I admit it'd be much tidier if I didn't love you, but I do." He gave her a rueful smile. "And I hope you feel the same. But love, as I'm sure you know, isn't enough. There's safety to consider, and our respective careers to balance. That means making allowances."

"I know," she said. "But I'm not going to break the law for Evan O'Malley, no matter how nicely he asks."

"You weren't breaking the law tonight," he said.

"Yeah, but we traded favors," she said. "It's a slippery slope, you know that. Next time it'll be something a little closer to the line. He's going to keep maneuvering, keep pushing, trying to get me to cross over."

"I agree," Carlyle said.

"What's the endgame here?" she asked. "This isn't going to work forever."

His hand moved down her wrist. He laced his fingers into hers.

"Nothing lasts forever," he said. "But I'll stand by you through this trouble, whatever happens."

Erin saw the softness in his eyes and believed him. But she knew softness wasn't enough to deal with what they had coming.

"I need to ask you something," she said.

"Go on, darling."

"If you have to choose, them or me, what's it gonna be?"

He didn't flinch or waver. "If it comes down to it, I'm with you."

She knew she should lay it on the line, right then and there, challenge him. If there was a chance to pull him out of the Life, she should take it. Right there, in that moment, seeing nothing but love and trust in his face, she thought he'd do it if she asked him.

But she didn't ask. Because if he tried to leave, they'd kill him. Seeing Mickey Connor face-to-face left her with no doubt whatsoever about that. She wouldn't ask him to lay down his life for her. That wasn't fair. And she wasn't sure she could live with herself if something did happen to him.

"Okay," was what she said. "That's what I needed to hear."

"Grand. Are you wanting a refill?"

She looked down at the whiskey glass and saw it was empty, though she didn't remember drinking most of it. "Yeah, thanks. But I can't get too drunk."

"You're off-duty, aren't you?"

"Yeah, but I got invited to go out to a bar with some of the fellas from work. At six in the morning."

Carlyle laughed. "My pub doesn't serve alcohol at such an ungodly hour. It's against the law, or so I'm told."

"Apparently this place does," she said. "It's a cop bar, gets the guys just off the night shift."

"Are you planning on staying up, or getting some sleep?"

"I'm too old to stay up all night, unless there's a damn good reason."

"Then I'll not keep you long," he said, getting up and pouring another drink from the bottle of Glen D.

"That's not what I meant," she said. "If you don't mind, I could crash here for a few hours."

"On the sofa?" he inquired, glancing at the piece of furniture she was sitting on.

She smiled. "I don't think so."

She hadn't stayed over at his place before, and she hadn't meant to suggest it now. It had just slipped out. "If you've got a spare toothbrush, that is."

"You're in luck," Carlyle said. "I know a lad." He set her drink on the coffee table, then leaned over and kissed her. She wrapped her hands around the back of his neck and pulled him toward her. There'd be plenty of time for bed. Right now, the couch suited her just fine.

Chapter 16

Erin hadn't set an alarm, but she was used to waking up early. She opened her eyes and saw a ceiling that wasn't hers. Then she remembered where she was. She rolled over and saw Carlyle, asleep beside her. She leaned on an elbow and studied his face. In sleep, the carefulness that was so much a part of his persona had dropped away. He looked younger, less worn and wary.

She wondered how he'd ended up on such an opposite path from her own, and how they'd wound up at the same destination in the end, lying on silk sheets upstairs from a pub. And she wondered how it was going to end. She'd been telling the truth the previous night. Their relationship wasn't going to work forever, not the way it was. Sooner or later, someone in the NYPD would tumble to it. Sooner, if Lieutenant Keane from Internal Affairs came sniffing around. Then there'd be hell to pay.

The thing was, Erin was having a hard time caring about the future just then. She felt like she was exactly where she was supposed to be. Being with Carlyle felt right. He was the first man she'd dated who really understood her, understood the Job, and didn't expect her to be anything but who she was. They could talk, really *talk*. Added to that was the crackling sexual chemistry. What woman wouldn't jump at the chance?

That was what Michelle, her sister-in-law, would say. But then, Michelle had two grade-school kids, brought up on a steady diet of happily-ever-after cartoons. Some of that optimism had rubbed off on Shelley. Erin saw all the bad things people did to one another, and they did some of the worst things to people they claimed to love.

Still, she couldn't deny she felt happier here than anywhere else she could've laid her head. She leaned over and very gently kissed Carlyle's cheek. He shifted slightly, but didn't wake up. She decided to let him sleep. Easing her way out from under the covers, she went looking for her clothes. Some of them hadn't made it all the way into the bedroom. She picked up her blouse from the coffee table in the living room and brought it back, along with her other things. Getting dressed in yesterday's clothes wasn't something she particularly enjoyed, but she didn't have a lot of choice. Going out in one of Carlyle's shirts would attract more attention than a wrinkled pair of slacks.

As she pulled on her pants, she glanced up and saw Rolf in the doorway. He was watching her with an unreadable expression on his face. She was probably reading too much into it, but he looked a little judgmental. It was the sort of look her father might have given her.

Her father. God, what was she going to tell him?

"Nothing," she muttered. "Not yet."

It was a little before six. She could be at the Final Countdown in fifteen minutes if she hurried.

"Hard liquor before breakfast," she said to Rolf. "Hey, who can say no to that?"

*   *   *

The Final Countdown was a little brick storefront. She found it just down the street from the Precinct 5 house. A CLOSED sign hung in the door, but as she peered in the window, she saw movement inside. A moment later, Piekarski opened the door.

"Hey, glad you made it," she said. "C'mon in. We just got here."

The SNEU team had a table in the middle of the room. A couple of other officers were at the bar. Logan stood up and raised a glass.

"Here she is! Woman of the hour!"

"Have a seat," Janovich said. "And a drink."

"I'm going on duty in less than two hours," she said. "I can't get hammered."

"Just one, then. On Firelli."

The Final Countdown didn't have Glen D whiskey, of course; Erin didn't know any bar but the Corner that carried it. She settled for Jameson.

"Still up, hey?" Piekarski said.

"What do you mean?" Erin asked. She took a sip. Whiskey before breakfast was not really what she wanted, but it was definitely an experience. Hard liquor on an empty stomach always was.

"Same outfit," the other woman said, nodding toward her.

"Oh. Right. No, I haven't been home yet."

"Maybe I oughta be a detective," Piekarski said.

"You'd hate it," Janovich said. "Too much paperwork."

"We got too much paperwork already," Firelli said.

"You're just sayin' that 'cause you're illegitimate," Janovich said.

There was an awkward pause.

"You know, illegitimate," Janovich said. "You can't read."

"Jan," Logan said, "there's so much wrong with what you just said, I don't even know where to start."

"Seriously, O'Reilly," Firelli said. "You should come work with us. Forget about that Major Crimes bullshit. SNEU is where the action's at."

"It's not bullshit," Erin said. "Well, not all of it, at least. Hey, I stopped a major terrorist attack last fall."

"Blah blah blah," Piekarksi said, winking at Erin as she mimicked her. "Look at me, I stopped a terrorist attack last year. Ain't I something? Bullshit. What've you done lately?"

"We take down hard felony collars every day," Logan said. "Hell, after we processed the guys from our bust, we did a couple 10-75Vs and nailed two more pushers with a buy and bust. And that was a slow night for us."

A 10-75V was a vertical patrol, which was when a police unit moved in the stairwells and hallways of an apartment building. A lot of the older apartments in the city had resident drug dealers. "Thanks for the invite," she said. "But I think I'm good where I am."

"How 'bout your partner?" Piekarski asked, offering Rolf her hand. He sniffed it in a businesslike manner and permitted a brief scratch behind the ears.

"He's not narcotics-trained," Erin said. "Explosives, human detection, and standard Patrol work. And he stays with me. You can have my dog when you pry his leash out of my cold, dead fingers."

"We could use a dog, Sarge," Piekarski pressed. "How do we get one?"

"Paperwork," Logan said with a wicked gleam in his eye.

Firelli and Janovich groaned.

"Maybe it's just as well," Firelli said. "If we got another Irish on the squad, it'd mess up Mickstat."

"But seriously," Logan said. "We owe you one, O'Reilly. It worked out to twelve kilos of heroin, ninety-six percent pure. That's over a million wholesale. If they step on it and cut it down, we're talking ten to fourteen mil, street price. Those two guys are going away for a good, long time. And a lot of junkies will be going cold turkey."

"Does it do any good?" Erin asked.

"We still got job security, if that's what you're wondering," Piekarski said.

"I need to bounce," Erin said, standing up. "Thanks for the drink, fellas."

"Keep the streets safe," Firelli said.

"If you insist," she said. "Turn around and put your hands on the bar. You have the right to remain silent..."

The rest of her Miranda warning to Firelli was drowned out by the laughter of the rest of the squad.

* * *

Erin didn't have time for her usual morning run, so she took Rolf for a quick walk, grabbed a shower, and swung by the bakery on her way into work. Stereotypes aside, a police officer couldn't go far wrong bringing a box of donuts with her to the office.

Vic and Webb were already there. Vic was finishing boxing up the last of the case files. Webb was at his computer, twirling an unlit cigarette in his hand while he worked on one of their reports.

"Morning," Webb said. "Nice to have an early night for a change?"

Erin thought he was being sarcastic until she remembered he didn't know about her excursion with SNEU. She briefly weighed telling him, and for complicated reasons decided not to.

"I had a good night," she said instead. "I brought munchies."

"You got the jelly-filled kind?" Vic asked, hurrying over and reaching for the box.

"I dunno. I just grabbed the usual box set."

Vic popped the lid and examined the merchandise. "If I get one that's filled with lemon, I swear, I'm gonna shoot the baker," he said.

"Please don't boost the murder stat," Webb said.

"Not in the head," Vic said. "I was thinking maybe the leg or something."

"We all set with the Bianchi case?" Erin asked, picking out a donut for herself and going to the break room to get a cup of coffee.

"In your dreams, O'Reilly," Webb said. "I sent you your part of the reports. There's the arrest report on Nina, the rest of the paperwork on Paulie, all the DD-5s, of course..."

Erin thought about what the SNEU team had said about joining up with them. It was actually a tempting thought for a moment.

"Okay," she said. "I guess it beats being shot at. So we're closed, other than the paperwork?"

"Yeah," Vic said. "They kept Paulie overnight, but they released him this morning, when the DA finalized the deal. He goes home free."

"He didn't kill anyone," Erin reminded him, not liking his sulky tone. "All he did was small-time, incompetent drug deals."

"He accidentally got Ridgeway killed," Webb said.

"A lot of other people helped make that happen," Erin said. "So Lorenzo finally got sick of his wife and decided to kill her. He poisoned a box of chocolate and left it out, knowing she had a sweet tooth. But by sheer bad luck, it was the same brand of candy Paulie and his Mafia buddies were using to hide their drugs. So Paulie gave the wrong box to his buddy Rocky, who actually did open it up later on, and found out it was exactly what the label said."

"Can we arrest Rocky?" Vic interjected.

"For what?" Webb asked. "All he did was eat some candy and give the rest to his girlfriend."

Vic shrugged. "He was supposed to get a box of drugs. I kinda feel like we should arrest him."

"Later," Webb said. "Guys like him always step in shit again. I'd bet a month's alimony he's behind bars before the end of the year."

"Anyway," Erin went on, "after Rocky snacked on some of the candy, he got the idea to give the rest of it to his girl. Unfortunately for Norman Ridgeway, he was screwing around with Rocky's girl, and she decided to share Rocky's candy with her other boyfriend."

"Not cool," Vic said.

"Of course, Ridgeway was also cheating on Hayward," Erin added. "Not that that makes it okay. But the poisoned almond nougats finally found a home, and that was it for Ridgeway."

"At least he died happy," Vic said.

"I'm gonna put that on your tombstone," Erin said.

"I said it before, I'll say it again," Vic said. "I love your optimism. You actually think you're gonna outlive me."

"I've seen your diet," she said. "You'll have diabetes before you're forty."

"But at least I'll die happy," he repeated, grinning.

"And that's it for the case," Webb said. "I expect the Narcs will want to keep an eye on Paulie and Rocky, hoping they'll lead them to bigger fish, but that's out of our court."

"Too bad," Vic said. "I was hoping we could bust that greasy Italian asshole."

"Better officers than you have tried," Webb said. "I've been reading up on our friend Vinnie. He's a slick son of a bitch.

They'll collar him on RICO eventually, I expect, but that'll be up to the Feds."

"The Feebies couldn't collar their own ass with both hands," Vic muttered, giving the usual NYPD opinion of the FBI.

"But regardless..." Webb began. He was interrupted by the phone on his desk ringing. He pivoted his chair and picked up the receiver. "Webb here."

Erin and Vic saw his face change. He looked disbelieving, then shocked, then tired, in rapid succession. "Copy that," Webb said. "Yeah, I understand. Who called it in? *Who?* Okay. Yeah, I'll send someone." He hung up and sagged back in his chair. "God damn it."

"Sir?" Erin asked.

"What the hell happened?" Vic asked.

"Paulie Bianchi went home," Webb said. "When he went inside his family apartment, someone was waiting for him. They put two bullets in the back of his head."

"He dead?" Vic asked.

Webb gave him a look. "You know many guys who live through two in the head? Of course he's dead."

"When did it happen?" Erin asked.

"Sometime in the last half hour," Webb said. "You'll never guess who called 911."

They waited.

"Rocky Nicoletti," Webb said. He went over to see his buddy, found the door open, Paulie on the floor with his brains, such as they were, spread out around him."

"I'm a little surprised Rocky called the cops," Vic said.

"You think Rocky's the one who shot him?" Erin asked.

"Could be," Webb said. "But I don't think even that kid's dumb enough to shoot his buddy and then call us. We'll check him for gunpowder residue to make sure."

"You want me over there?" Erin asked.

"Nah, you stay put, O'Reilly," Webb said. "I'll go with Neshenko. He deserves to get out of the office every now and then. Besides, we're not going to make an arrest."

"How do you know?" Vic asked.

"This was a Mob hit," Webb sighed. "The guy who did it is long gone, with an alibi already in place."

"I don't get it," Vic said. "Why whack Paulie? He was nothing, just a small-time piece of shit."

"Maybe someone thought he knew something," Webb said. "Unfortunately, we can't very well ask him."

Erin stopped listening. Her mind was spinning as she realized what had happened. "Oh God," she said.

"Erin?" Vic said. "You okay? Shit, Lieutenant, she's gonna faint!"

"No, I'm not," she said, but for a moment, she'd felt the donut and coffee trying to come back up. They'd arrested Paulie Bianchi on a drug charge. Then, just a few hours later, the NYPD had busted a significant heroin shipment meant for Bianchi's people, and she'd told SNEU it was on a tip. Then, the following morning, who'd walked out of jail, free and clear? From a mobster's perspective, it couldn't have been clearer. Vinnie the Oil Man had interpreted events the only way he could, and arrived at the logical, if incorrect, conclusion. And he'd taken the action any good Mafia don would.

"You sure you're okay?" Vic asked. "You looked like a goddamn ghost."

"You sick, O'Reilly?" Webb asked, looking at her with concern.

"No, I'm fine," she said. "It was Vinnie. He's our guy."

"No shit," Vic said.

"Not that we'll be able to prove it," Webb added. "Damn, I hate these cases. Even when we know who had it done, we can't nail them. Mob hits are the worst. Come on, Neshenko. Count yourself lucky, O'Reilly. We're just going to go through the motions, I'm afraid."

Erin nodded numbly, still trying to untangle what she could and couldn't tell her fellow detectives.

Chapter 17

Webb and Vic trailed back into Major Crimes three long hours later. Erin was plugging away at her DD-5s, trying to pretend she wasn't thinking about Paulie Bianchi. Rolf was napping on his blanket next to her desk.

"Got anything?" she asked, a little too quickly.

"The Lieutenant's got jack," Vic said, "and I've got shit to go with it."

"No witnesses," Webb said. "The weapon was a nine-millimeter automatic, two shots. Levine says the shots were almost contact close, entrance wounds just behind the right ear, powder tattooing around the wounds."

"Execution-style," Erin said.

"Exit wounds took off half his damn face," Vic said. "Hell of a mess. Closed casket for sure."

"Looks like the shooter was waiting for him behind the front door," Webb continued. "He came in and didn't even have time to see the guy. Probably never knew what hit him. CSU's going over the scene, but it looked pretty clean. Professional."

"And we got no motive," Vic added.

"Of course we have a motive," Webb said. "Someone must've told Paulie's boss he'd talked to us, cut a deal."

"Nina's the one who cut the deal," Erin said.

"That's a fine distinction," Webb said. "We should've had protection on Paulie." He sighed. "Damn it, I should've guessed this would happen. I just figured Paulie wasn't important to anyone but his mom. I got tunnel vision."

"We all screwed up," Erin said.

"Speak for yourself," Vic said. "My conscience is clean as a newborn baby."

"Newborn babies come out kind of slimy," Erin said. "And covered with blood."

"Okay, bad example," Vic said. "But I didn't kill this idiot, and I didn't get him killed. We know Vinnie Moreno had him killed."

"We *suspect* that," Webb corrected. "But I don't see any other reasonable theory. And unlike Lorenzo Bianchi, Vincenzo Moreno *is* the subject of a RICO investigation."

"I don't believe it," Vic said. "You're throwing this one to the Feebies? Jesus, boss, this is a New York homicide!"

"RICO is the only way to stick a higher-up with a hit like this," Webb said. "There'll be three layers of insulation between Vinnie and the triggerman. Unless the Feds flip someone in the chain, there's no way the Oil Man takes the rap for this."

"So that's it?" Erin said. "Not our case?"

"Not our case," Webb agreed. "I don't like it either, but we've got no choice."

"It'll take five years," Vic grumbled. "And then they'll get him on some sorry shit like tax evasion."

"That worked on Capone," Webb reminded him. "So unless you're requesting a transfer to the FBI's White Collar Crime program, Neshenko, we're packing it in. We'll send our files to the FBI and call it good."

Erin said nothing. She told herself it didn't matter why Vinnie thought what he did; what mattered was that he'd had Paulie killed. And there wasn't a damn thing she could do about it. She stood up. Rolf, always attentive, bounced to his feet and wagged his tail.

"Where you going?" Vic asked.

"I gotta take care of something," she said.

"Police business, or personal?" Webb asked.

Both, she thought. "Personal," she said.

Webb shrugged. "It's about lunchtime anyway. Can you be back in an hour?"

"Sure. What've we got going?"

"It looks to me like you're not quite done with your paperwork," he said.

"That's because I'm illegitimate," she said. She left the office while Vic and Webb were still staring at her, trying to figure out what the hell she was talking about.

* * *

Erin drove to the Barley Corner, not even knowing what she was going to say when she got there. Her thoughts were a haze of guilt and confusion. Rolf, picking up on her mood, shifted uneasily in his compartment and whined softly.

She parked in the police space outside the pub and went in, walking fast. The Corner was filling up for the noon rush, and she didn't see Carlyle right away. Caitlin was up front. She grinned at Erin.

"Hey, Erin," she said. She'd had a soft spot for Erin ever since a gang of hitmen had attacked the Corner while she'd been there. Erin and Carlyle had fended them off while Caitlin and Danny had huddled behind the bar.

"Hey," Erin said. "Your boss around?"

Caitlin pointed. "Usual spot."

"Thanks." Erin threaded the crowd and saw Carlyle. His face lit up when he saw her, and he got up from his barstool.

"Hello, darling," he said.

"We need to talk," she said.

He saw it in her face. "What's happened?"

She glanced around and saw half a dozen guys who might be Mob-connected.

"Upstairs," she said.

He nodded and led the way to the back stairs, ushering her through the door and making sure it locked behind Rolf. They went up to the living room, where Rolf sat beside the couch and watched them.

"Do you want anything?" he asked, gesturing to his personal drink cabinet.

Erin shook her head. "They killed Paulie Bianchi this morning," she said bluntly.

Carlyle froze in the act of reaching for a whiskey bottle. "Who?"

"Paulie Bianchi!" she snapped impatiently. "Sewer Pipe's kid!"

"Nay," he said. "I meant, who killed him?"

"Vinnie the Oil Man."

He nodded. "I see."

"No, you don't," she said. Then the words came out in a flood, so quickly she could hardly control them. "We cut a deal with his mom, so she confessed to killing Lorenzo. Lorenzo was trying to kill her first, but everything got screwed up and the stupid dentist ate the candy, and now Lorenzo's dead, and Nina's in jail, but Paulie walked on the drug charge, which would've been fine except for your asshole buddy Liam and his goddamn tipoff. Then I hit the drug shipment with the street Narcs, and Vinnie figured the only way we'd have known was if

Paulie had talked, and there he was, getting let out of jail like he'd made the deal himself. So bang bang, that's it for Paulie."

Carlyle walked slowly over to Erin and put a hand on her shoulder. She shrugged him off.

"Erin, darling," he said. "Paulie Bianchi worked for the Mafia. They're a suspicious lot. They don't need to prove guilt beyond a reasonable doubt. Doubt's quite sufficient for them to act. They killed him."

"I got him killed," she said.

"Are you weeping for the lad?" Carlyle asked quietly. "He was a petty criminal, a dealer in narcotics. I believe your lads would call this a 'misdemeanor homicide.' Paulie was in the Life."

"You're in the Life!" she shouted at him. "What am I supposed to do if you get whacked?"

He shook his head. "I'm a bit more experienced than young Paulie," he said. "I know my way around these lads."

"That makes you safe?"

"Not safe," he said. "But a little safer, aye."

"This case," Erin said. "Jesus Christ. It's just such a chain of screw-ups, beginning to end. It started with the wrong guy getting killed, and now it's ending the same way."

"Who's the right guy?" Carlyle asked.

"Your buddy Liam, and whoever the source is who gave him the tip on the drugs," she said. "He's got someone in Vinnie's organization, someone important."

"More than likely," he agreed. "Would you feel better if Liam was the one lying on the ground with a few extra holes in him?"

"I feel shitty either way," she said. "I got a shady tip, acted on it, and a guy got killed. What the hell does it matter who it was? Shit, I guess I'm in the Life now, too."

Carlyle's face hardened. "Don't say that," he said. "Don't even think it. Don't ever say that, unless you want it to be true. I love you, Erin, and if it came down to it, I'd take bullets for you. You know that. If being with me drags you down, you'd best walk out that door and never come back, because I'd not forgive myself."

"But you won't stop being a gangster," she said.

He gave her a slight, sad smile. "It's not as easy as all that. If I walk away, now of all times, when I've just gotten involved with a copper... Well, darling, didn't you just come to me with an example of what can happen?"

"You wouldn't be betraying them," she said stubbornly.

"Did Paulie betray his people?" Carlyle replied. "Erin, you need to remember, in this world, the truth matters less than most people think. It's the perception that matters."

Erin nodded. "We're screwed, aren't we?"

Carlyle actually laughed softly. He put his hand on her shoulder again, and this time she softened to his touch.

"Darling, if you know anyone on this earth who isn't, be sure to point them out. I don't know if you've noticed, but not a one of us is getting out alive."

"Don't you dare get yourself killed," she said. "Because if you do something stupid and get whacked, I swear, I will drag you out of your coffin and kill you again. And if you think I'm leaving you to deal with these assholes alone, you're out of your damn mind."

"Erin, have I ever told you how much I appreciate your romantic sentiments?"

Seeing his poker face as he said it, she couldn't help it. The tension broke and she fell against him, laughing almost hysterically. He put his arms around her, and she held him in return.

"We'll figure it out," he said after a few moments.

"More people are gonna die," she said.

"If they do, that's not on you," he said. "All of us make our choices and have to live with the consequences."

"Or not live with them," she added. "You know, this whole thing would be a lot easier if I didn't love you."

He pulled back to arm's length. "You've not said that before," he said. "Is it true?"

Erin smiled shakily. "This would be a pretty lousy time for us to start lying to each other."

"I'm not Lorenzo Bianchi, you know," he said. "And you're not Nina. We're writing our own story, with our own ending."

"You don't get to choose how your story ends," Erin said grimly.

"Sometimes," Carlyle said, "when you come down to it, that's the only choice we have left."

Author's Note

I wish to acknowledge a debt to Edward Conlon of the NYPD for his excellent memoir "Blue Blood." I am particularly indebted to him for his lively and compelling accounts of the inner workings of the New York Police Department's Street Narcotics Enforcement Unit.

Here's a sneak peek from Book 8: Massacre

Coming 2020

Erin saw the smoke from three blocks away, rising over lower Manhattan. As she got closer, she was able to follow the flashing lights of squad cars, fire engines, and ambulances. The street was choked with emergency vehicles. Lights, sirens, and blaring horns overwhelmed her senses. Poor Rolf, with his sensitive ears, was having an even worse time.

Erin parked as close to the scene as she could. She got Rolf and dismounted, making her way toward the billowing smoke. She didn't see Lieutenant Webb, but she noticed the Bomb Squad van in front of the building and angled that way. A young guy with a military buzz cut was standing next to the van, talking to an engine captain from the Fire Department.

"Hey, Skip!" she called, recognizing her friend.

"Hey, Erin!" Skip Taylor replied. "You might want to keep back a little. Fire's still going."

"I can see that," she said. She turned to the firefighter. "Sir, what's the situation?"

"Firebombing," the captain said. He pointed to the front of the building. Dense clouds of smoke poured through the shattered plate glass. "Excuse me, Detective. I know you have your job to do, but right now, I have mine. We're containing the blaze. I've got Engine 24's crew working the fire, and 55 doing a rescue search."

"They're inside?" Erin asked, appalled. As a first responder, she'd made entry to burning buildings, but it was never safe or easy.

"Yes, ma'am," he said. "Excuse me." He turned and went quickly toward the fire.

"What can you tell me, Skip?" Erin asked the bomb tech.

"I was just talking to the cap about the danger of secondaries," he said.

"Secondaries?"

"Secondary explosions," he explained. "We've shut down the gas lines, and I'm guessing they don't have propane tanks inside, so the worst I'd expect would be a grease fire. The guys should be okay."

"O'Reilly!"

Lieutenant Webb hurried over, Vic Neshenko looming behind him. Erin's commanding officer had his trademark unlit cigarette in one hand. Webb looked unhappy, even by his standards.

Vic, on the other hand, was cheerful. "Welcome to the party," he said.

"What've we got?" she asked.

"Dispatch got a 10-10S," Webb said, the code for a crime in progress with shots fired. "We had a Patrol unit less than a block away. When they rolled up, they took fire from at least two automatic weapons, so they fell back and called for backup."

"Any officers hit?" Erin asked sharply.

"Nope," Vic said. "Lucky bastards. Got some holes punched in their car."

Erin suppressed a shiver, remembering a similar situation she'd been in last year. "Glad they're okay," she said.

"While they were pinned down, some joker tossed a Molotov through the storefront," Webb continued. "Then the perps took off around the corner. They must've had a car waiting. Backup arrived in less than two minutes, but the shooters were already gone."

"Traffic cams?" Erin asked.

"No good," Vic said. "We'll check 'em, but there's a lot of traffic on that road, and we don't have footage in the middle of the block, so we don't know which car was theirs. We may be able to ID the shooters at the corner, but we'll have to run all the plates on all the cars."

"And theirs will be stolen," Erin predicted. "They've probably already dumped the car."

"Probably," Webb gloomily agreed.

"How many shooters?" she asked.

"The uniforms saw three," Vic said.

"We've got spent brass all over the sidewalk," Webb said, indicating the front of the building. "Of course, New York's Bravest are contaminating the hell out of the crime scene as we speak. I hate arson jobs."

"On the bright side," Vic said, "the shooting ended before we got here."

"You're in a good mood," Erin observed.

"Can't a guy be happy?"

"Not if it's you," she said. "I'd call that highly suspicious."

"You gotta watch out, Erin," he said. "All this time around crooks and psychos is making you paranoid."

"It's not paranoia..." she began.

"...if they're out to get you," he finished. "Hey, Lieutenant, how long you think they're gonna take hosing down our crime scene?"

"Depends on what they find," Webb said. He was starting to say something else when a distinctive sound cut through the controlled chaos on the street. A series of loud pops, it was immediately recognizable to anyone who knew it.

Erin and Vic had their sidearms drawn before they'd even fully registered what they'd heard. Skip, who'd served in combat in Iraq, was even faster. He was crouching behind his van's engine block by the time Erin shouted, "Shots fired!"

"Where the hell did that come from?" Webb demanded, drawing his old service revolver. Cops and firefighters were scattering, taking cover and looking frantically for the shooter. More shots rang out.

"Over there!" Vic shouted, pointing at the burning building.

"You've got to be kidding," Erin muttered.

The fire captain ran toward Webb, a radio at his ear. "Lieutenant!" he shouted. "I've got men inside taking fire! I have a man down! I need cover!"

"Get me masks and fire gear," Webb snapped, energizing. He waved over the nearest Patrol officers. "I need some volunteers. We've got men in there who need help."

There was the briefest hesitation. Then a young officer whose nametag read RUIZ stepped forward. "I'll go, sir."

"I'm in," Vic growled. Two more shots came from the building. Everyone but Vic flinched.

"Let's do it," Erin said. Turning to the captain, she quickly asked, "Is it safe for my K-9?"

"Can he do SAR?" the captain replied.

"Yeah," she said.

"Then we need him. Let's move!"

The police grabbed firefighter overcoats and oxygen tanks on their way. Erin was trying not to worry about Rolf. He was absolutely willing to go in, and being low to the ground, he wouldn't have as much to fear from smoke inhalation as the rest of them, but he wouldn't be able to stay inside long. "*Komm,*" she ordered, giving the command in his native German. He trotted beside her, alert and attentive.

"You better stay outside, sir," Erin told Webb. He tended to get short of breath at the best of times.

"You giving me orders, O'Reilly?" he retorted. "I've been sucking smoke since I was sixteen. I'm used to it."

Ruiz looked very young, and very scared, but he buckled on his gear with steady hands. The four officers formed up outside. Even through the protective gear, Erin could feel the heat of the fire, like an open oven door.

"Let's go," Webb ordered.

"NYPD!" Erin shouted as they plunged in. "Sound off, guys! Where are you?"

The fire made a strange, hollow roaring sound. Everything was smoke, heat, and flickering flame. Erin heard the rasp of her own breathing in the oxygen mask. The smoke was disorienting. Even though they were barely inside, she had trouble remembering the way out. Strange shapes of tables and chairs appeared and disappeared through the smoke. If anyone answered her call, she didn't hear them.

"Rolf!" she ordered. *"Such!"*

Hearing his "search" command, the K-9 moved forward, sliding with his belly close to the floor. How he could smell anything but smoke was a mystery, but he was clearly on the scent of someone. Erin held his leash in one hand, her Glock nine-millimeter in the other. She was in the lead, the other officers keeping close so as not to lose contact.

Rolf suddenly stopped and scratched the floor. Erin saw a body at her feet. She knelt and saw it was a man, dressed in street clothes, face down. Blood was pooled around him. He didn't seem to be breathing, but it was hard to tell.

"Got a casualty!" she shouted. Even as she said it, a sustained burst of gunfire came from very close at hand.

"Christ!" Vic said. He snapped off two shots in return.

"Don't fire blind!" Webb barked. "You out there! This is the NYPD! Put down the weapon and give up! You're going to die in here! We're here to help you, idiot!"

"Fire Department!" someone shouted to Erin's left. "We got a man down!"

"Rolf!" Erin repeated. *"Such!"* She nudged him in the direction of the voice.

Rolf was off again, sneezing and snorting. Erin went with him, keeping as low as she could. Another gunshot sounded, followed by two more from Vic.

"God damn it, Neshenko!" Webb shouted.

Erin found an overturned table, a looming shape in the smoke. Behind it, three firefighters were huddled with a fourth one at their feet. The wounded man was writhing in pain.

"We'll cover you!" Erin shouted.

Ruiz was behind her. He tapped her shoulder to let her know he was there. He rested the barrel of his pistol on the edge of the upturned table. "Go!" he said.

Erin and Rolf moved back the way they'd come. The firefighters followed, carrying their downed buddy. No more shots were fired. Erin dared to hope Vic might've gotten lucky. Or maybe the shooter had gone down from smoke inhalation, or suffered an outbreak of common sense and just stopped shooting.

The police and firefighters tumbled out of the building onto the sidewalk, into blessed fresh air and sunlight. It was a cold early-March day that Erin thought had never felt so good. They pulled off their masks and sucked in the air. Rolf, at her side, gave a wheezing cough and sank to the pavement.

Ready for more?

Join Steven Henry's author email list
for the latest on new releases, upcoming books and
series, behind-the-scenes details, events, and more.

Be the first to know about new releases in the Erin
O'Reilly Mysteries by signing up at
tinyurl.com/StevenHenryEmail

About the Author

Steven Henry learned how to read almost before he learned how to walk. Ever since he began reading stories, he wanted to put his own on the page. He lives a very quiet and ordinary life in Minnesota with his wife and dog.

Also by Steven Henry

Ember of Dreams
The Clarion Chronicles, Book One

When magic awakens a long-forgotten folk, a noble lady, a young apprentice, and a solitary blacksmith band together to prevent war and seek understanding between humans and elves.

Lady Kristyn Tremayne – An otherwise unremarkable young lady's open heart and inquisitive mind reveal a hidden world of magic.

Robert Blackford – A humble harp maker's apprentice dreams of being a hero.

Master Gabriel Zane – A master blacksmith's pursuit of perfection leads him to craft an enchanted sword, drawing him out of his isolation and far from his cozy home.

Lord Luthor Carnarvon – A lonely nobleman with a dark past has won the heart of Kristyn's mother, but at what cost?

Readers love *Ember of Dreams*

"The more I got to know the characters, the more I liked them. The female lead in particular is a treat to accompany on her journey from ordinary to extraordinary."

"The author's deep understanding of his protagonists' motivations and keen eye for psychological detail make Robert and his companions a likable and memorable cast."

Learn more at tinyurl.com/emberofdreams.

More great titles from Clickworks Press

www.clickworkspress.com

The Altered Wake
Megan Morgan

Amid growing unrest, a family secret and an ancient laboratory unleash long-hidden superhuman abilities. Now newly-promoted Sentinel Cameron Kardell must chase down a rogue superhuman who holds the key to the powers' origin: the greatest threat Cotarion has seen in centuries – and Cam's best friend.

"Incredible. Starts out gripping and keeps getting better."

Learn more at clickworkspress.com/sentinel1.

Hubris Towers: The Complete First Season
Ben Y. Faroe & Bill Hoard

Comedy of manners meets comedy of errors in a new series for fans of Fawlty Towers and P. G. Wodehouse.

"So funny and endearing"

"Had me laughing so hard that I had to put it down to catch my breath"

"Astoundingly, outrageously funny!"

Learn more at clickworkspress.com/hts01.

Death's Dream Kingdom
Gabriel Blanchard

A young woman of Victorian London has been transformed into a vampire. Can she survive the world of the immortal dead— or perhaps, escape it?

"The wit and humor are as Victorian as the setting... a winsomely vulnerable and tremendously crafted work of art."

"A dramatic, engaging novel which explores themes of death, love, damnation, and redemption."

Learn more at clickworkspress.com/ddk.

Share the love!

Join our microlending team at kiva.org/team/clickworkspress.

Keep in touch!

Join the Clickworks Press email list and get freebies, production updates, special deals, behind-the-scenes sneak peeks, and more.

Sign up today at clickworkspress.com/join.

CPSIA information can be obtained
at www.ICGtesting.com
Printed in the USA
BVHW081843100822
644244BV00004B/636